"The wealth management industry is being redefined as we speak. While robo-advice will drastically change how financial institutions serve mass-affluent clients, goals-based wealth management is becoming the golden standard for high-net-worth firms. Paolo Sironi's book provides a holistic and comprehensive look at these complex industry changes."

–Alois Pirker, Research Director, Aite Group

"*FinTech Innovation* is a FinTech survival guide for anybody who manages, invests or saves money. Disruption in Asset Management is coming fast and this book highlights how to benefit from innovation such as Robo-Advisory and Goal Based Investing. This is a must-read book by Paolo Sironi, a global FinTech Thought Leader!"

–Susanne Chishti, CEO, FINTECH Circle; Chairman, FINTECH Circle Innovate; Co-Editor, *The FINTECH Book*

"This is a thoughtful and superbly executed look at how financial technology has brought welcome changes to the world of investment management. This is essential reading not only for next generation investors but all investors who want to fully understand how money - their money - will be managed going forward."

–Mark Landis, Founding Partner, Wavelength Capital Management LLC

"Paolo Sironi succinctly captures FinTech's role in the escalating disintermediation of the Wealth Management industry, while offering a logical rationale for what may lie directly ahead. The convergence of investment advice and planning via potential real-life simulations will create a new path for Global Wealth Managers. Goal Based Investing may very well offer regulatory and revenue solutions for a rapidly changing industry."

–Mark Cipollina, Executive Director, Head of Investment Advisory UK, Standard Chartered Bank

"This book presents a bold new vision on Fintech and Goal Based Investing! Just in time for the largest wealth transfer in history. Goal Based Investing and FinTech solutions are in the minds of every millennial and baby boomer who is millennially-minded."

–April Rudin, CEO/Founder, The Rudin Group

"It's simple. If you want to know what the future holds for wealth management, ask Paolo Sironi. His latest book presents a personal vision of financial advice that all market participants must heed to stay relevant, and ultimately to stay in business."

–Aki Ranin, FinTech blogger and Entrepreneur

"This book presents a masterly account of the shifts in the digitalization of financial services and wealth management seen from the perspective of a bank, advisor and investor."

–Anthony Christodoulou, Founder, Wealthtrack – Robo-Investing Europe

"Paolo Sironi takes us beyond the hype to remind us that FinTech Innovation is about customer outcomes. This book provides insights on how quantitative finance and digital technologies can be combined to change the way the wealth management industry can help consumers achieve their goals."

–Stephen Huppert, Partner, Deloitte Consulting

"Paolo Sironi's book courageously addresses a transformation that is just starting to happen. Before the dust settles, he captures the essence of the shift from plain vanilla auto-investing to the next generation. He offers a qualitative and quantitative framework that can address the issue holistically: Goal Based Investing with Gamification elements. A strategic solution that Sironi examines from both sides of the spectrum: the financial services provider and the end-user point of view."

–Efi Pylarinou, Founding Partner, Daily Fintech

FinTech Innovation

From Robo-Advisors to Goal Based Investing and Gamification

PAOLO SIRONI

WILEY

This edition first published 2016

Registered office
John Wiley & Sons Ltd, The Atrium, Southern Gate, Chichester, West Sussex, PO19 8SQ, United Kingdom

For details of our global editorial offices, for customer services and for information about how to apply for permission to reuse the copyright material in this book please see our website at www.wiley.com.

Library of Congress Cataloging-in-Publication Data

Names: Sironi, Paolo, author.
Title: Financial innovation : from robo-advisors to goals-based investing and gamification / Paolo Sironi.
Description: Chichester, West Sussex, UK : Wiley, 2016. | Series: The Wiley finance series | Includes bibliographical references and index.
Identifiers: LCCN 2016011452| ISBN 9781119226987 (hardback) | ISBN 9781119227182 (epub)
Subjects: LCSH: Financial services industry—Technological innovations. | Finance—Technological innovations. | Financial engineering. | BISAC: BUSINESS & ECONOMICS / Finance.
Classification: LCC HG173 .S54 2016 | DDC 332.6—dc23 LC record available at https://lccn.loc.gov/2016011452

A catalogue record for this book is available from the British Library.

ISBN 978-1-119-22698-7 (hardback)   ISBN 978-1-119-22719-9 (ebk)
ISBN 978-1-119-22718-2 (ebk)   ISBN 978-1-119-22720-5 (obk)

Cover design: Wiley
Cover image: Charts image: (c) Sergey Nivens/Shutterstock; Plant image: (c) Romolo Tavani/Shutterstock

Set in 10/12pt Times by Thomson Digital, Noida, India

To my champion and the beloved creatures of my family

Contents

Preface

So far, most of my professional life has been spent at the intersection between **FIN**ance and **TECH**nology, whose line of separation has recently been blurred by financial technology companies (FinTechs). The forces that are fostering their innovative mindset are unveiled in this book, which closely scrutinizes the revolution occurring in the wealth management industry, and particularly digital advice, personalized investing, and cognitive analytics being used to give insight into the behaviour of customers. The findings are based partially on market research and academic material, but mostly on what I owe to the hundreds of business conversations with industry leaders, innovators, entrepreneurs and colleagues. They have enriched this book, transformed any business travel that I have undertaken into a scholarly opportunity, and ultimately made my humble career, which started in risk management, an invaluable journey. Back in the 1990s, I learned to implement advanced quantitative methods to manage trading risks and I engaged periodically with top managers and regulators in search of graphical yet robust simulation methods to turn complex mathematical equations into intuitive reporting. When the wind of innovation blew at my door in the early days of the FinTech revolution, I was easily led on an entrepreneurial journey, it was my goal to change the investment experience as it existed between financial advisors and their respective clients, to allow them to speak more comfortably the intuitive language of Goal Based Investing (whose quantitative foundations are demonstrated in my previous book *Modern Portfolio Theory: from Markowitz to Probabilistic Scenario Optimisation*). I then had the privilege and deep learning opportunity to engage with the extensive network and client base of IBM on a global scale. This contributed to refining the strategic thinking at the heart of this book about the many challenges that small and large wealth management firms face in a disrupted landscape made of technology developments, generational shifts, changes in investors' behaviour, tighter regulation, and declining revenues in the traditional models of financial advice. Wealth managers do stand at the digital epicentre of a tectonic fault, which is disrupting their landscape that has, in many ways, been unchanged for centuries.

On the institutional side of this fault, FinTechs have been building new business models, such as automated investment services, that compete fiercely with established banking operations. There is an ongoing debate about the future of the industry and the chances of FinTechs to disintermediate incumbent organizations fully. Whether they will settle in as the new leaders, or will die like a bee after expending its sting, cannot really be divined and is not the primary scope of this book. We are not siding either with David or with Goliath. What we are instead concerned with is any innovation that can transform the investing experience to benefit each and every one of us, the community of taxable investors and their human or digital financial advisors. As a matter of fact, FinTechs have already won the first round of the innovation battle, as incumbents have started to update their business models and compete in a challenging race to zero prices. Robo-Advisors, for example, were born as "garage companies" using digital tools to on-board customers and enhance their experience to disintermediate retail and private banking relationships. They also developed advanced technology to operate automated portfolio rebalancing, to squeeze trading costs to a minimum, and disintermediate the role of asset managers.

On the other side of the fault, the community of end investors is also shifting in response to technology trends which are transforming social behaviour globally. Not only Millennials but older generational cohorts are embracing with unforeseen facility all aspects of the digitalization of everyday life. From a wealth management perspective, their willingness to become more digital in handling their investments has further lowered the barriers to entry.

The transforming forces at play inside this fault are unprecedented. The offer-side has always dominated the wealth management relationship because financial institutions had unrivalled placing power with private clients. They could team up with product factories, such as asset managers and desks of capital markets, to embed hefty fees into financial products, collect them from final investors, and redistribute them among institutional players. The loss of reputation suffered by these players during the Global Financial Crisis (GFC) has seeded the regulatory terrain with new legislation, which is breaking the financial services' cartel in favour of final consumers, by raising fiduciary standards and enforcing greater transparency. While the offer-side is becoming progressively a "constrained offer-side", the community of investors is granted the flexibility to disintermediate centuries-old banking frameworks with relatively easier to understand investment experiences, any time, anywhere, at a much lower costs. This process of digitalization of the banking relationship is encouraging the demand-side (private clients) to take a more conscious and proactive role, empowering individuals and with them their personal financial advisors or digital intermediaries, and threatens to relegate wealth management institutions to lower margin business models.

The epicentre of this figurative earthquake is indeed located in the process of remodelling the **asymmetry of information**, which has always characterized the relationship between institutions and final clients, and kept the tectonic fault between them stable. This is now being pulled apart! The community of investors, intermediated by smart and tech-savvy financial advisors, can now become the new price-makers and force banks to be price-takers as part of a global process of **banking democratization**.

The book takes us on a journey below the disrupted surface of the wealth management industry, providing insights into what happens in its underlying layers. Deep within the crust, digitalization and demographic changes coupled with social media and Big Data analytics are colliding against established economic interests. Yet, this seismic activity is not just unsettling the technological and business landscape around but is also creating new minerals, a process known by scientists as flash evaporation. **Goal Based Investing** (GBI) is the resulting gold mine enriching the fault zone and is permitting early adopters of robo-technology to transform disruption into sustaining innovation. The theory of innovation provides a framework that helps to explain where the forces of change originate from, what is happening in the marketplace, and how the industry can evolve once robo-technology becomes mainstream.

Pre-eminently, Goal Based Investing seems to be the new normal in investment management as it provides a solution to fee-only businesses attempting to showcase their added value. Although such an investment philosophy is not new in economic studies, the industry has never truly felt compelled to realign to its best practice imperatives: traditional sales models have long proven that product-driven organizations were profitable. Moreover, technology constraints did not previously allow the building of the right customer experiences and make GBI principles effectively engaging. But this has now been solved by the usage of application programming interfaces (APIs), new digital tools, and faster than ever computing power. Furthermore, **Gamification** is emerging as a new digital force in the wealth management ecosystem. Goal Based Investing can provide the consistent mindset to gamify investments by simulating personal goals, market scenarios, and life events to enforce more adequate investment behaviour.

Discussing new methods (Goal Based Investing) and developing new solutions (automated rebalancing, API analytics, Gamification) might not be sufficient to enforce industry change if the economic incentives don't remodel as well within the firms themselves. In the present day widespread market regulation about fiduciary standards is facilitating a realignment to sounder client/portfolio-centric approaches. This enhancement is not cost free, and it requires a change of perspective from a traditional asset management point of view (optimization of the market variables) to a more personalized investment modality (elicitation of investors' ambitions and fears over time). In such a transforming environment, in which investors' fears and their long-term aspirations take centre stage, GBI principles will gear financial advice and financial planning to converge, and thus allow customization of the investment offering around clients' ultimate goals, generating premium services to tier and drive profitability (hence sustaining innovation). GBI robo-winners will be best placed to outpace laggards, whether FinTechs or digital incumbents.

Organization of the book

Individual investors, financial advisors, portfolio managers, technology and digital managers, banking executives, and FinTech entrepreneurs can gain strategic insights about the transformation of the wealth management industry by reading this book and understanding the links between new technology and quantitative finance, as well as adapting to a tighter market regulation and higher fiduciary standards. Technology experts will learn about the rationales behind the many requests and challenges addressed to them by business owners. Financial professionals will learn how new technology can transform their business models and advisory workflows. To help facilitate this learning journey the book is organized into three parts:

- (Part One) Personalize Personal Finance
- (Part Two) Automated Long-Term Investing Means Robo-Technology
- (Part Three) Goal Based Investing is the Spirit of the Industry

Part One – Personalize Personal Finance

The **first and introductory chapter** presents a high-level model for banking transformation and refers to the theory of innovation, which is the rationale that links disruptive technology (Robo-Advisors and automated rebalancing) and sustaining innovation (Goal Based Investing and Gamification). Today's disruption is threatening a variety of market participants and goes beyond the fate of human advisors: ETF providers, mutual funds, active funds and platforms are all primarily affected. While digitalization lowers the barriers to entry and reduces intermediation margins, Goal Based Investing allows us to personalize and differentiate the investment offer to increase revenues, and thus calibrate to the clients' requirements by means of social and behavioural analytics.

Part Two – Automated Long-Term Investing Means Robo-Technology

The second part opens with the **second chapter** of this book, which provides a non journalistic definition of Robo-Advisors and a discussion about their strengths and weaknesses. They have five main attributes: they are automated digital businesses, they promote passive investing, they provide automated portfolio rebalancing and tax optimization, they engage customers on personal goals and behaviour, and they are single minded businesses.

The **third chapter** examines the changes in the marketplace, with particular reference to the offer-side of the supply-demand mechanism. All actors involved in the industry are affected by these changes, which Robo-Advisors seem to exploit. The chapter looks into the future of robo-advice and explains how tech-savvy financial advisors can use indexation and robo-technology to their competitive advantage. They can use algorithms for "alpha" generation (that is model portfolios provided by automated rules) and focus on "gamma tasks" to justify their fees (that is human added-value advice and financial planning). Financial advice and financial planning begin to converge, as Goal Based Investing leads the way.

The **fourth chapter** focuses on mega trends affecting the behaviour of the demand-side, made up of the variety of private and taxable investors. Since Millennials and Baby Boomers are shown to interact differently with digital media, financial advisors can learn to optimize their practices by tiering the clientele on digital and goal-based groups: clients' triage is no longer a function of disposable wealth but a function of their personality and techno-literacy.

The **fifth chapter** summarizes the most compelling dilemma of the wealth management industry and sketches the potential outlook of a highly digital supply-demand chain. The key factor is the personalization element, hence the usage of robo-technology to facilitate a holistic Goal Based Investing approach to financial well-being.

Part Three – Goal Based Investing is the Spirit of the Industry

The third part is therefore dedicated to Goal Based Investing and Gamification.

Part Three opens with the **sixth chapter** of the book, which describes Goal Based Investing (GBI) as the ultimate step in personalization within the journey of wealth management innovation, which sits at the crossroads between classical portfolio theory and behavioural finance. Individuals seem to make investments according to their mental state at a particular time, hence they exhibit multiple goals, multiple priorities, multiple investment horizons, and multiple risk tolerances. The probability of achieving/missing a target becomes the key analytics to generate and discuss in a GBI compliant investment policy.

The **seventh chapter** features a quantitative discussion about the most common approaches of portfolio modelling, which have been adopted by the first generation of Robo-Advisors. Alternative solutions are also featured, such as Probabilistic Scenario Optimization (PSO), to strengthen GBI implementation, allow for graphical representations of past and future performance, guide investors and advisors in making consistent decisions of portfolio rebalancing, and provide a framework for scenario analysis and quantitative Gamification.

The **eighth chapter** provides further insights about Gamification, which is more art than science, but seems to provide a chance to support a behavioural finance effort to rewire investors' brains towards a sounder investment engagement, by means of exposing them to gamified investment experiences.

Finally, the author gives his **concluding remarks**, certain that the readers can by then appreciate – albeit not necessarily share – all the theories, evidence, and reasoning that this book provides.

Acknowledgments

I am sincerely grateful to the numerous clients, colleagues, and friends who, knowingly or unknowingly, have enriched my whole professional life. In particular, I owe thanks to Thomas Martin who has provided continuous feedback and constructive criticism to shape some of the ideas featured in this book, and to Anil Suri who has rewarded me with open conversations during my NY travels, which also refined my vision about Goal Based Investing and Gamification. I am also grateful to my colleagues at IBM Risk Analytics, my professional family in the broader IBM, for their incessant dedication, and Wiley's editor Thomas Hyrkiel, for believing in this thought leadership project. Most importantly, I am indebted to my family, who love me and helped me dedicate time to this work.

This book contains thoughts, strategic views, and opinions which have forged the professional background of the author but are the author's only; these do not necessarily represent the practice nor the views of my current or previous employers, nor the beliefs of my present and past colleagues.

Paolo Sironi, 2016

About the Author

Paolo Sironi is a recognized author of books about portfolio management and FinTech innovation. In his current role as IBM thought leader for Wealth Management and FinTech Analytics, Paolo links FINance and TECHnology globally, demonstrating sound expertise over a number of areas including Wealth Management, Asset Management, Risk Management and Financial Technology.

Prior to IBM, Paolo founded a FinTech startup (2008) to provide Goal Based Investing solutions to wealth managers. The startup became a part of IBM (2012) following the acquisition of funding partner Algorithmics, a world leader of risk management solutions.

Paolo has a decade of risk management expertise; he was previously head of market and counterparty risk modeling at Banca Intesa Sanpaolo.

Paolo's posts can be read on LinkedIn, Twitter: @thepsironi or his personal website: thepsironi.com.

PART One

Personalize Personal Finance

CHAPTER 1

The Theory of Innovation: From Robo-Advisors to Goal Based Investing and Gamification

"People don't want to buy a quarter-inch drill. They want a quarter-inch hole."
—Theodore Levitt (1925–2006)

This chapter sketches the main arguments of this book. The theory of innovation provides the framework that helps to explain why robo-technology (disruptive) and the gamification of Goal Based Investing (sustaining) sit together as key determinants of today's banking transformation. The search for personalization is the *fil rouge* that links the main elements of wealth management innovation. Industry decision-makers are therefore addressed with some useful action items, which allow them to tackle with clarity and rationality the challenges of robo-technology transformation.

1.1 INTRODUCTION

The history of banking is clearly the history of money, hence the history of trade which can be traced back as early as 12,500 B.C. to the usage by Anatolians of obsidian, a raw material used to build stone-age tools. But banking, as we know it today, is a more recent industry which was forged during the 12th century and early Italian Renaissance to facilitate commerce and manage personal finance for wealthy families in rich cities such as Florence, Venice, and Genoa; Monte dei Paschi di Siena being the oldest bank operating continuously since 1472. During the 17th and 18th centuries North European cities such as Amsterdam and London took the lead, fostering systemic innovations like central banking. Yet, only during the 20th century, and especially after the industry deregulation in the 1980s, which saw New York and London emerge as world leading financial centres, has financial innovation enabled banks to stretch their balance sheets and grow the level of international interdependence to the point of becoming a potential systemic threat to the stability of modern economies, as demonstrated by the unfolding of the Global Financial Crisis (GFC) in 2007.

Given the global scale of the banking industry, the interdependence between finance and technology has also grown steadily because information technology (IT) has facilitated the harnessing of economies of scale. For many decades banks have been front runners in IT spending. This has followed regulatory pressure to strengthen their fast growing operations, but also a need to compete and adapt to more efficient technology frameworks with the motto "invest more to save more". Notwithstanding, today's digitalization shift has revealed that most banking systems are still obsolete and leave the industry exposed to unexpected competition: small FinTechs, financial technology companies, are imposing themselves against traditional models by using digital technology as a weapon to tear down the barriers of entry and potentially disrupt the whole industry.

Technology is not the only force in motion to transform financial services. Regulation is clearly the other major driver affecting existing business models, if not the leading force. Widespread criticism has hit established banking practices in the aftermath of the GFC, alerting international regulators to the importance of strengthening the rules of conduct of the intermediaries to protect the interests of individuals and the community of investors at large. Transparency, adequacy, and suitability have become the major leitmotifs for compliance officers. But most importantly, the ban on retrocessions and the required transparency about costs and fees, as well as the rise of personal financial advisors, have started to hinder established business models which seemed too rigid to embrace change. Existing incentive schemes based on product selection have become inconsistent with a global push towards added-value and fee-only investment services. This is clearly a threat to the sustainability of banks' balance sheets, because it severely impacts the sustainability of cost/income ratios. Banks are required to increase their IT spending to transform digitally, while intermediation margins are shrinking and economic capital has become scarce and very expensive. Yet, from a high-level perspective, such an increase in the cost of capital has pushed many institutions to reduce their investment banking and proprietary desks, and forced them to look at wealth management operations more strategically (Goldman Sachs being one of the few exceptions). This repositioning of banks' portfolios can be the opportunity to transform this ancient industry, and enable private investors to take centre stage in the investment process by starting from the eliciting of their ambitions and fears, hence by personalizing the investment process to their individual needs and abandoning the more generalist asset management point of view. This shift is a change of perspective from the analysis of market variables (e.g., expected return, variance, Sharpe ratios) towards client-centric representations of investment goals (e.g., probability of achieving targets), which goes under the name of Goal Based Investing. As a matter of fact, it is not surprising that most of the FinTechs operating in the domain of personal finance have adopted rudimentary GBI schemes to design their disruptive investment propositions: they anchor the investment dialogue to personal goals and time horizons that match individuals' personal traits.

> *"But are FinTechs truly disruptive? Is banking about to be unbundled? Would regulators favour this shift in the long term, or would they oppose it given considerations of financial stability?"*

Disruption is effectively underway, though it might take the form of transforming existing firms more than putting them out of business by the rise of Robo-Advisors. However, not all firms may be able to transform, so that there will be winners and laggards, which may well be forced out of the game. Clearly, no future can be predicted for any industry, nor the fate of any individual company. But the theory of innovation can provide the mindset to explain the transformation at play by revising, and helping to understand, the most common reasons that lead companies (e.g., banks) to go out of business, no matter how dominant they were or how much skill their respective management possessed at the time of downsizing. The remainder of this chapter is dedicated to discussing what FinTechs do, dissecting the principles of innovation theory, and explaining why robo-technology, Goal Based Investing and Gamification directly relate the one to the others.

1.2 A VIBRANT FINTECH ECOSYSTEM

FinTechs are start-up companies which appeared between 2008 and 2010 particularly in the US, not confined to Silicon Valley creative capabilities, but fast spreading out to the East Coast, Europe, Hong Kong, Singapore, Australia, and much of Asia. The FinTechs' ecosystem features a variety of business propositions which can span from peer-to-peer lending to digital payments or Big Data analytics. Yet, if we look at the business philosophy and aspirations of their founders, we can draft a quick and dirty definition that links their most common ambitions: digitalization, analytics, specialization, and long-tail consumers. We can therefore refer to them as follows:

> *"FinTechs are a global phenomenon, born at the intersection between financial firms and technology providers, attempting to leverage on digital technology and advanced analytics to unbundle financial services and harness economies of scale by targeting long-tail consumers."*

Clearly, digitalization plays a key role, because digital tools allow the creation of captive customer experiences as weapons to tear down the barriers to entry in financial services, hence fostering borderless competition against established institutions. Most of today's FinTechs make usage of analytics to generate competitive business propositions in terms of marketing, positioning, social media, and handling of Big Data. They feature a high level of specialization, hence very narrow and simple

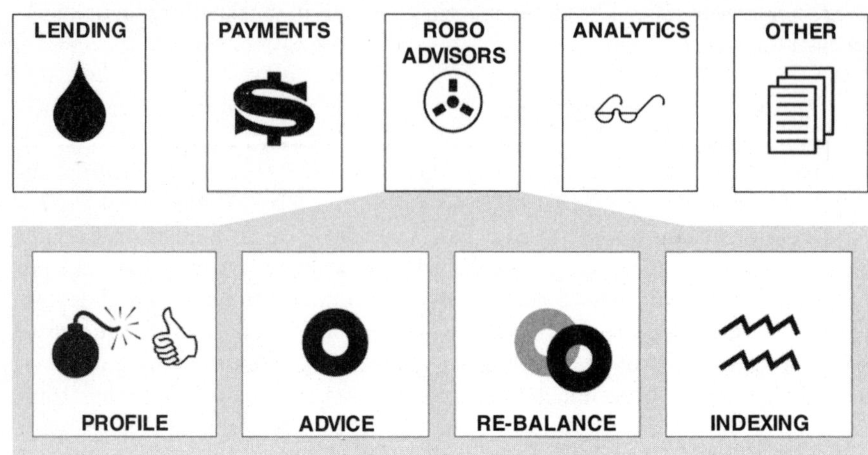

FIGURE 1.1 FinTechs high-level classification

business propositions, to profit from a concerted attempt to unbundle financial services into leaner and specialized digital offers. Finally, they target directly or indirectly long-tail consumers to disintermediate established providers with cheaper services. Typically, they are Business to Consumer firms (B2C), but Business to Business (B2B) and Business to Business to Consumer (B2B2C) models are emerging to fill the void between starlight innovators and the need of financial institutions to transform fast. The FinTech *parterre* changes very fast and is populated by new firms and ideas almost every quarter. Hence, we refrain from commenting on individual cases: such an exercise of market intelligence would be the focus of research analysts, whose thorough work has also kindly inspired the drafting of this book and helped to navigate through the variety of species fighting for affirmation within this ecosystem. By and large, they can be classified as in Figure 1.1: retail lending, payments, analytics, personal finance, and residual models.

Peer-to-peer retail lending solutions and digital payments seem to be the offers with stronger disruptive power. This can be due to the protracted credit crunch cycle in developed economies (following the GFC) and the astonishing growth of shadow banking in growth markets, as well as their appeal to established brands in social media and technology (e.g., Alibaba, Apple, Facebook, and Google), capable of intercepting money flows and direct consumer spending by means of behavioural analytics. Social media and digital technology are affording the opportunity to leverage virtual networks among individuals, without the need for traditional intermediaries. Potential creditors can reach out “almost directly” to potential debtors, by pooling in small ticket investments to lending facilities specialized in personal lending or small corporate. Although an exciting application of the synergies between finance and technology, there is mounting concern among international regulators about the soundness and sustainability of the players operating in shadow banking as these businesses thrive outside traditional channels regulated by international supervisory bodies.

As a matter of fact, cryptocurrencies are a rising and highly debated phenomenon at a time when world economies are running progressively on paperless cash, which can be used and transferred online. Mobile and wearable are granting IT firms unprecedented power to disintermediate centuries-old banking centrality of cash repository and payment services, and help to foster financial inclusion in poor countries. As telecommunications and the world wide web have become fairly ubiquitous, we can nowadays visit smarter cities and pay-per-use the underground using a smartphone instead of holding physical travel cards, carrying a credit card or unloading spare change out of our pockets. In this domain, blockchain technology has the potential to be truly revolutionary.

The internet has favoured the global acceptance of social media and granted innovators with a fertilized terrain to develop advanced analytics which identify, analyse, and target investors' preferences, and track their digital interaction and peer-to-peer relationships. Big data analytics, behavioural analytics, and cognitive computing operate in this space. FinTechs are given the opportunity either to adopt these techniques as part of their operations or to create new business models that provide analytics-driven services, such as digital assessment of personal credit risk.

FinTechs operating in the domain of personal finance are also on the rise. One of the main consequences of the GFC has been a tightening of international regulation to increase the cost of capital and foster investor protection. Although regulation is not always an even playing field across constituencies, we can clearly see a global trend towards the increase of fiduciary standards and suitability constraints, affecting the economic relationship between product factories (e.g., asset managers) and final advisors. This has ignited the rise of Robo-Advisors, which use digital tools to attract private money across the continuum of the clientele, promoting low fees and tax harvesting, typically built on passive investments or portfolio algorithms that threaten asset and wealth managers.

Finally the FinTech ecosystem is enriched by more models which we refer to as residual simply because they do not yet reach the headlines as much as the other players and are somewhat less numerous in each bucket. This is the case of FinTechs providing market or economics research, dealing with encryptions, password storage, or broader digital security.

Within this variegated ecosystem, Robo-Advisors are the game changers of personal finance and the main focus of this book. Most of the professional debate we can follow on social media and read in the financial press refers to the advantageous price point of Robo-Advisors, which is often a fraction of the cost that private investors face by accessing traditional banking. However, while the price battle may be short-lived, the aspect which provides them with long-term strength and which is fostering industry-wide transformation resides in their advanced user experience (UX). Final investors are often seduced by an investment experience which seems to be more personalized when compared with traditional e-trading solutions. Notwithstanding, we must be aware that most of the underlying investment processes which existing Robo-Advisors hide behind their catchy UX are instead somewhat institutionalized, as they are based on a limited number of model portfolios compared with the larger variety of individuals' needs and characteristics. Personalization elements are key drivers of most FinTechs and sit at the top of the agenda for digital banking. Goal Based Investing has to do with truly personalized investment decisions.

1.3 SOME DEFINITIONS, LADIES AND GENTLEMEN

Robo-Advisors are new digital experiences addressing personal finance whose elements of innovation are primarily discussed in this book. This first chapter discusses more general principles of banking innovation, concentrating on wealth management transformation. Therefore, it seems useful to anticipate some concepts of the remaining chapters and define what Robo-Advisors, Goal Based Investing, and Gamification are.

First, **Robo-Advisors** are automated investment solutions which engage individuals with digital tools featuring advanced customer experience, to guide them through a self-assessment process and shape their investment behaviour towards rudimentary goal-based decision-making, conveniently supported by portfolio rebalancing techniques using trading algorithms based on passive investments and diversification strategies. These digital businesses differentiate by degree of passive management, depth of investment automation, interaction between human advisors, and level of self-assessment, as well as target clientele.

Second, **Goal Based Investing** is an investment philosophy which places the individual at the centre of the investment decision-making process. The true risk that individuals face is not market volatility but the probability of falling short of personal goals. Therefore, the approach is a true game changer because it requires greater interaction between the advisors, human or digital, and final investors to elicit more consistently their risk tolerances as well as their ambitions and preferences over time.

Third, **Gamification** refers to the use of engaging gaming mechanisms to modify the behaviour of individuals. We refer to new innovative ideas which relate not solely to the need of engaging clients through their digital life and guide them to visit the virtual premises of a digital bank, but mainly to the possibility of educating final investors about the perils and biases related to financial investments. Thus, help them to rewire their brains and mitigate some well-known biases identified by behavioural finance and prospect theory to avoid making inconsistent decisions (e.g., buy high and sell low).

Robo-Advisors, Goal Based Investing, and Gamification are the three pillars of this book and represent different elements of innovation in the field of personal finance. Robo-Advisors' ecosystem is evolving fast, transforming from B2C businesses towards B2B2C Robo-4-Advisors (hybrid solutions made up of technology and human advice) and B2B Robo-as-a-Service. Goal Based Investing principles are not a new phenomenon, but only recently have they gained momentum because of a mix of regulatory tightening to favour transparent fee-only businesses and the effective availability of digital technology to institutionalize their added value beyond the exclusive circles of family offices. Gamification experiences were born well before robo-advice was first launched, but they have not expressed their full potential yet to transform the way people invest and interact with digital solutions.

Much effort is spent in searching for greater automation, fancier mobile design, and customer analytics. This is part of an industry effort to face the wind of change brought about by the social and technology mega trends which are sweeping the world: a generational shift, the Internet of Things, growing social media lives, cognitive computing disruptive potential, and Big Data analytics. What links these elements together is the search for personalization.

1.4 PERSONALIZATION IS KING

Robo-Advisors have been hitting the headlines and attracting everyone's attention in a frenzied search for the next unicorn. We are not going to add to the debate around single propositions, believing that the wealth management market is not a "winner takes all" game. As such, we are more concerned with the elements of technology and business innovation which operate in the background, some shared by many while others are slightly more specific. The main essence of Robo-Advisors resides in their attempt to institutionalize the "personalization" of the investment experience, hence adopt Goal Based Investing (GBI) principles which they have rudimentarily exemplified, consciously or not. GBI is the most likely new normal to shape wealth management operations in the decades to come, because its principles represent the spirit of the industry, if not simple common sense, and its message is clearly well aligned with the whole essence of banking regulation: to transparently service clients' interests by placing their ambitions and fears to the centre stage of any advisory relationship. Who could possibly disagree? The fact is that banks are profit-orientated organizations which operate in regulated environments whose rules are devised to protect the interests of individuals and the community at large, if not national economies.

Yet, the asymmetry of information between professional bankers and private or corporate customers has always granted financial institutions an unrivalled pricing power. In fact, this has pushed wealth management institutions to optimize their cost/income ratios in the short term, instead of the long-term interest of their respective customers. The GFC has shown that this behaviour was not forward looking. The change in approach, which requires a shift from asset management centrality to a client-centric vision, is not an easy journey though. Firms need to revise their incentive structures, their organizations, their business models, and legacy systems which are currently not fit for purpose. However, as digitalization becomes a must, today's technology allows us to take a significant step forward and institutionalize the private banking relationship to make it economically convenient for boutiques as well as larger retail institutions. Robo-Advisors, although still infants in their adoption of GBI principles, have already moved in this direction. Their robo-features might have stolen the innovation scene but the revolution that they have truly ushered in, consciously or not, is about the adoption of quick and dirty GBI principles by using behavioural finance as a way to engage clients and personalize the investment relationship: that an investor risk profile is attached to its goals, that an investor ambition is instrumental in achieving a personal target which can change over time, that time is the continuum along which fears and ambitions need to be combined into rebalanced portfolios are all key elements of Robo-Advisors' on-boarding of new clients. Aren't they also GBI principles?

The personalization mantra is therefore paramount and places Robo-Advisors at the forefront of the Goal Based Investing landscape. As financial institutions suffered a severe loss of reputation during the GFC, the asymmetry of information that once dominated the financial services industry started losing strength, after its peak with the adoption of the supermarket banking model. Regulatory changes and new customer behaviours (particularly those of Millennials) have made the banking relationship less sticky in favour of higher flexibility on the side of final investors. The banking industry has recognized the strategic value in providing tailored investment propositions. Advisory campaigns need to be calibrated on a different triage technique, as customers react to advisory proposals not just as a function of their wealth, but also their social behaviour and tech-savviness. Big Data analytics and behavioural analytics, strengthened by the development of cognitive computing, seem to grant FinTechs and banking institutions the chance to remodel their business setups along these lines. Yet, banking is a highly regulated industry and investing has different psychological implications from spending. Therefore, analytics need to be carefully fine-tuned to encompass the revolutionary findings of behavioural finance and possibly the biology of risk. Robo-technology facilitates the deployment of modern analytics to redesign the advisor-to-client relationships on more balanced and added-value methods of portfolio choice, helping to institutionalize the principles of Goal Based Investing to benefit affluent and mass affluent clients, outside the exclusive circles of family offices (as in Figure 1.2). Banks had already started a digitalization journey of their retail operations, only to realize as they were progressing how relevant and strategic this would also be to better service the relationships with wealthier clients. Private bankers can make use of digital innovation to deploy cost effective goal based conversations, which now become accessible to lower tiers of the wealth pyramid.

We consequently ask ourselves if Robo-Advisors are truly disruptive within the digital landscape, and draft the principles underlying the theory of innovation as they can help us to read through most of the evidence and reasoning provided in the remaining chapters. Let's shape our mindset first! We will then explain in detail how Robo-Advisors work.

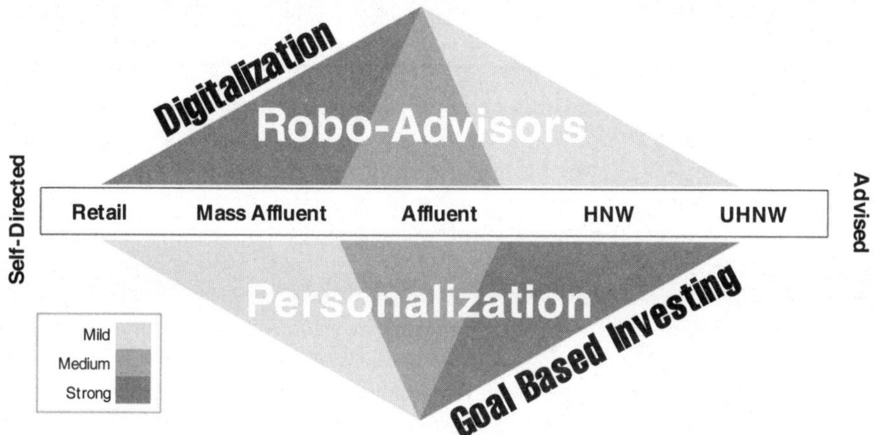

FIGURE 1.2 Digitalization and Goal Based Investing

1.5 THE THEORY OF INNOVATION

Robo-Advisors are automated portfolio rebalancing solutions whose investment style typically conforms to passive management and which private investors can invest into by using digital tools, featuring clients' engagement modules with customers' behaviour and personal goals at the cornerstones of their propositions. Much of the recent media coverage about FinTechs describes Robo-Advisors as disruptive players against more traditional incumbents.

"Is robo-technology truly disruptive?"

The theory of innovation can help us to articulate a reasonable answer and distinguish between two key concepts: technology and innovation. First of all, we define technology as any process by which a firm transforms information and data, human labour or economic capital into products or services of greater value. Therefore, digital advice, automated portfolio rebalancing, and Goal Based Investing workflows could all be defined as technology. Second, the introduction of new technology modifies the way firms operate or customers access services and products. Technology is a process which evolves over time, both inside and outside individual firms. Therefore, we define innovation as any change in existing technology used by a firm, and recognize that such a change can take two forms: disruption or sustaining growth. Sustaining innovation refers to improvements in product performance, whether of an incremental nature or more radical, that allows one to increase the quality of firms' offer, fend off competition, or increment commercial margins, by operating either on lower costs or on higher prices. Disruptive innovation instead might well result in worse product performance, at least in the near term. Such revolutionary products are usually cheaper, simpler or more convenient to use and appeal to new customers or create new needs in existing clientele. This book grants equal relevance to both components, with a certain discontinuity from mainstream theory. Disruption is not an overnight event, and its economic advantages are truly sizeable only when new technology has a clear path ahead to generate further improvements, hence sustaining innovation, and thus higher margins. Robo-Advisors are classified as disruptive innovation because they are cheaper than traditional financial advice, they are simpler to access, they appeal to new customers, and create a new need among existing clientele. Goal Based Investing, whose principles Robo-Advisors seem to have rudimentary adopted, is instead an example of sustaining innovation, which can offer the opportunity to move outside the unpleasant corner of low margins and achieve revenue growth over time, by providing tiered added-value services.

Traditional firms typically face two challenges in their lifetime: deciding how much investments need to be dedicated to sustaining innovation and, most importantly, recognizing that disruptive innovation can be the main cause of failure of established brands, although such innovation might seem to be anti-economical in the near term. Banks are not exempt from the need to answer this dilemma:

> *"How do sustaining and disruptive innovation interact to shape the future of industries?"*

Clayton M. Christensen (2002, 2003) proposed an insightful representation of this interaction, which we can re-edit in Figure 1.3, representing the relationship between innovation and industry/product performance (i.e., the quality of advisory services).

There seems to be a fixed amount of innovation that a regular customer can absorb in any industry, hence a capped amount of money that investors are willing to pay to receive better products or services. Clearly, not all investors are equally constrained due to different preferences or spending capability, which permits wealth managers to tier their offer across segments: retail, affluent, high net worth (HNW) and ultra high net worth (UHNW). Yet, as time goes by, industries evolve, technology changes, and so does investors' behaviour. Thus, markets or segments can saturate: no further innovation can lead to higher commercial margins. This is when disruptive innovation has the highest chance of succeeding. Initially, disruptive solutions are seen as a phenomenon confined to less appealing low margin clients (e.g., customers of retail banking) or distant markets (e.g., emerging economies). Yet, disruptive innovation can downshift the product paradigm globally, across markets and segments, so that customers start favouring the new solutions and move *en masse* towards new offers. This can put out established players who have no time to adjust their traditional workflows or business models. Market leaders become laggards and new entrants gain momentum (e.g., Apple vs. Nokia) and climb up the hall of fame of successful brands.

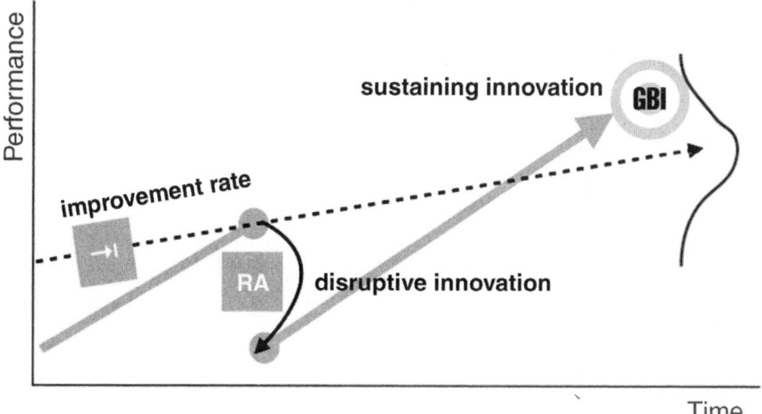

FIGURE 1.3 FinTechs high level classification

Thereafter, the cycle of sustaining innovation reignites and successful firms can strengthen commercial margins by improving once very simple disruptive products. It is worth noticing that nowadays the innovation cycle seems to be shorter than ever as new technology can be deployed faster.

1.6 MY ROBO-ADVISOR IS AN IPOD

To exemplify why Robo-Advisors possess elements of disruptive technology, we can discuss a parallel to the recent history of the music industry after the iPod was launched. The first Compact Disc (CD) player was sold in Japan by Sony in 1982. The CD levelled up the music industry by setting higher standards and inducing fierce industry competition by means of sustaining innovation. A period of tech spending involved a large number of consumers, who were buying new appliances offering higher levels of sophistication. Within a decade many households were equipped with advanced High Fidelity components (Hi-Fi) featuring equalizers, subwoofers, powerful amplifiers, and fancy headsets that parents were willing to buy to reduce late night noise. Soon, individuals reached a peak in consuming satisfaction, and in the late 1990s they could not possibly justify paying higher prices for a declining marginal improvement in music quality. The music market was saturated. Steve Jobs grabbed this chance and in 2001 launched the Macintosh version of iTunes and the first Apple iPod (think of a Robo-Advisor), six years after the MP3 was first introduced. The key selling point of the iPod was not better music quality compared to existing CD players. The fact was that the product was cheaper, more portable, and certainly cooler than CD players. Those who thought that it would have been a phenomenon confined to young consumers, walking up and down the streets with white cables in their ears, were proved wrong. The era of the Hi-Fi was over, the traditional way of buying and listening to music was disrupted and changed forever. Most importantly, today the dependence of Apple's revenues on iPod sales is very limited, as Cupertino entered a new wave of sustaining innovation to release higher margin services and devices, such as iPhones and iPads till the launch of the Apple Watch in 2015 (think of Goal Based Investing).

What does this tell us about the fate of wealth management? Digital trends are a mix of technology advances and changes in consumers' behaviour which are facilitating the creation of new entrants to compete with traditional firms. Robo-Advisors are FinTechs which have been attempting to downshift the advisory services that have always been the *apanage* of private banking institutions. They started to target retail investors needing financial advice, but lacking the resources to pay for the necessary human based services. With an entry level investment of circa US$ 5,000, Robo-Advisors were meant to appeal to low margin customers and mostly a very young clientele whose needs were unmet by traditional bankers, as they did not account for a large contribution to their balance sheet figures. Yet, Robo-Advisors proved to be very attractive solutions, not just for low income young customers, but also for affluent and high net worth mature individuals. Banks, already reconsidering their focus on wealth management operations due to the increasing cost of capital in investment banking, yet challenged by tighter market regulation, were quite abashed to see that new entrants were threatening their once dominant position, making the headlines of newspapers and attracting a considerable amount of venture capital money in a short time. This is why Robo-Advisors can feature as disruptive technology and relegate the banking industry to simpler and low income business models. Clearly, although new entrants have every interest in using digital weapons and dumping incumbents, neither the Robo-Advisors nor the financial institutions willing to transform have an interest in cornering themselves into lower income shops.

Goal Based Investing will provide smart players with a way out of the impasse. The tendency will be for financial advice and financial planning to converge within robo-models and this will allow tiering the offering to appeal to a more diversified client base, thus pricing up services by competing on more articulated added-value propositions (e.g., Gamification of Robo-Retirement). This leads to another key question:

"Will banks be disrupted?"

We cannot honestly say whether banking will be disrupted to extinction, or will transform under market and consumer pressure. However, the latter seems to be the most likely outcome, in our opinion, given the unique characteristics of banking to be a regulated industry and therefore being capable of reining in innovation and avoiding full disruption. The industry is clearly changing fast and robo-technology is certainly transforming the business landscape. What lies ahead is not a one-sided competition, FinTechs versus traditional firms, but a likely situation where a handful of digitally transformed actors could become the new dominant players, while traditional institutions unwilling to, or not capable of embracing change would become laggards. After all, banks are not eternal and of all the banks which dominated the Italian Renaissance, only one is still in business today (and it seems to be very troubled too).

1.7 WHAT INCUMBENTS SHOULD CONSIDER WHEN THINKING ABOUT FINTECH INNOVATION

What is left for traditional banks is a clear dilemma as to how to resolve the hurdles of fostering banking digitalization and adjusting their business models to keep up with shifts in customer behaviour. Some firms are creating on-the-side FinTech businesses to promote innovation outside mainstream banking, while others are more aggressively transforming their business models from the inside out. Some others are still hesitant to embrace digital change. Although inaction does not seem to be a forward-looking option, given the impressive forces at play in the industry, we acknowledge the difficulty even for seasoned managers to embrace all the complexities and risks that digital change can generate. The industry is not simply required to change parts of its IT configuration. Financial institutions need to transform their entire business model, and rectify the economic incentives which motivate all professional actors involved in banking activity while delivering existing traditional services. With particular regard to wealth management, the industry is changing from being a "distribution channel of financial products" into a "distribution channel of financial advice". This would correspond to a Copernican change in the way financial advisors operate and are compensated, which top management have to struggle with to make sure the firms they lead can transform without hindering existing profitability. No bullet-proof solution exists. Firms need to elaborate a proper multi-year strategy for innovation in order to operate with coherence yet promote new unexpected ideas. The theory of innovation can guide us in tackling some of the unknowns rationally. Decision-makers are invited to focus on the following five principles, as in Christensen (2002, 2003): the principles of resource dependence, of market irrelevance, of discovery based planning, of capabilities versus disabilities, and of the supply-demand gap.

The principle of resource dependence indicates that companies ultimately depend on customers and investors for resources, as these tend to exert moral suasion to prioritize their investments. In fact, firms that decide on investment patterns that do not satisfy them are more likely to be put out of business. This might well generate a Catch 22: as the leading companies are those that best match existing needs of customers and investors, they might also find it very difficult to invest in disruptive technology because the lower margins granted by these products do not appeal yet to mainstream operations. This can hold nicely, until customers' behaviour modifies and it becomes too late to embrace change. Our advice is for banks and asset managers to set up autonomous organizations outside their mainstream businesses, with the scope to research and build solutions around disruptive technology. They could also partner with venture capitalists to fund external vehicles, and grant them both adequate financial means and enough operational independence to succeed.

The principle of market irrelevance indicates that small markets don't solve the needs of large companies or, as can also happen, incumbents' business models do not fit certain markets. Disruptive innovation can occur in markets that seem too small or too distant to be attractive for existing and dominant organizations. This happened with Robo-Advisors, targeting retail consumers which were considered too "small" in terms of revenue potential to guide them through innovation. Our advice is that wealth and asset management firms instruct smaller organizations to innovate and commercialize new services in such markets, at least until market size becomes large enough to be embraced by the full arm's length of mother organizations.

The principle of discovery based planning indicates that markets that cannot be measured cannot be managed. Firms have learned to adopt market intelligence mechanisms as fundamental elements of decision-making: planning departments can access Big Data analytics to investigate market trends and make decisions about new services and products. Yet, disruptive innovation can occur in contexts where market research is of little use due to a lack of statistical evidence. Our advice to solve the gap is that decision-makers can run dedicated planning sessions in which they assume that established assumptions and forecasting data are wrong, and hence chosen strategies might be faulted. For example, the assumption that private investors can be tiered efficiently along the lines of disposable income, or wealth, has been contradicted by digital solutions which have shown that customers' ability to absorb banking services does not depend on wealth. Robo-Advisors have blurred the traditional triage, appealing to customers of retail banking as well as high net worth individuals, attracting clients on their techno-literacy and social media engagement. By restarting on clean assumptions, financial institutions can plan to learn what needs to be known, and can thus confront disruptive changes more effectively.

The principle of capabilities versus disabilities indicates that an organization's capability resides in its processes and values. When confronting change, firms might assign the most capable employees to direct change, yet adopt established values and processes which could instead conflict with what is really needed by disruptive innovation. Therefore, existing capabilities might prove to be damaging disabilities in new business contexts. This could be the case for firms willing to digitalize investment relationships by tackling the challenge from a pure IT perspective, thus replicating existing business workflows on digital mediums and missing the relevance of realigning incentive schemes and revising business practices as a fundamental part of the technological change. Our advice is that new capabilities need to be identified (e.g., professional profiles capable of blurring the line between technology and quant finance), and company values might also demand to be enriched to fit the purpose (e.g., allow for budgeting processes with shorter decision-making cycles or lower procurement constraints). Social media competences are skills in high demand in banking, as traditional firms might still struggle to adopt the personalized and engagement principles that social media requires to embrace successfully digital marketing and branding campaigns.

Finally, the principle of the supply-demand gap indicates that technology supply may not equal market demand. Often, sustaining innovation exceeds the rate of performance that consumers can possibly absorb. Hence, products that fit market demand today might evolve into overshooting solutions tomorrow, while underperforming products today (such as disruptive products) display the highest potential to showcase further sustaining innovation. Our advice is that wealth managers and asset managers revise their analytics to better measure trends of how their mainstream customers consume products and quickly catch the points at which competition changes the market they serve.

The presentation and re-editing of these five principles correspond to our humble attempt to guide incumbent decision-makers in starting their journey of transformation on the right foot. Clearly, no firm is equal to another. Some operate in more traditional markets, others have already created vehicles to foster innovation through direct banking, and quite a few of them have been flying their best resources first class to visit FinTech hubs and learn what they are all about, if not what might come up next. We do not necessarily indulge in a discussion about which of them (firm or business model) is better suited to emerge as a winner, nor which FinTech will survive the first five or ten years of innovation. But we invite financial institutions to get ready to act, because the time for change is now!

1.8 CONCLUSIONS

We have dedicated this chapter to outlining the main themes of the book, which aims to represent the changes that the wealth management industry is facing due to technology advances and shifts in customer behaviour. We have classified FinTechs according to their aspirations, as well as their business focus. More importantly, we have sketched the theory of innovation to guide us through the forces at play under the crustal plate of the wealth management industry. Next, we can delve into a deeper understanding of robo-technology, clear the table of journalistic representations, and examine the elements of competitive advantage which will shape portfolio construction practices for private wealth in the years to come. In the final part we will present the principles of Goal Based Investing and review related innovations in quantitative finance and Gamification.

PART Two

Automated Long-Term Investing Means Robo-Technology

CHAPTER 2

Robo-Advisors: Neither Robots Nor Advisors

"Carneades, who was he?"

—Alessandro Manzoni (1785–1873)

This chapter is dedicated to the innovation of Robo-Advisors. We clear the table of journalistic buzz about robo-technology and discuss what they really are, where they originate from, and how they are evolving. Their key points are explored: digital focus, single business mindedness, passive investment management, long-term portfolio rebalancing, effective on-boarding mechanisms, as well as tax-loss harvesting.

2.1 INTRODUCTION

Many of us enjoy our morning rites, reading a newspaper while toasting bread, drinking a cup of coffee before going to work. The youngest and most tech-savvy might scroll the latest tweets on global finance. Recently, there has not been a day without a new blog post about Robo-Advisors and their disruptive potential. This topic has clearly made an impact on professional media, although there seems to be a lot of journalistic biz-buzz around it, which might not facilitate a rational debate about the characteristics of these FinTechs.

We can just ponder for a moment the term "Robo-Advisor". This bloggers' term conveys a biased perception about what these companies really are and do. For the many tech enthusiasts, Robo-Advisors are fully automated machines which make investment decisions without any human interaction and can fully replace professionals to provide advice that eliminates any conflict of interests to benefit final investors. Many others instead focus on the perils of excess automation, and promote a sort of luddite juxtaposition between customer-committed human advisors and unmanned automated services. This book takes a more balanced stance and shows that techno-literate advisors have the most to gain from robo-technology. Digital-Advisors can use digital solutions to become more efficient in assessing, investing and reporting on clients' goals, thus saving time to focus on prospecting and added-value conversations. A way of disentangling from this conflict of minds would be to use a more appropriate appellation, such as "Automated Investment Solutions" (AIS). But we are aware that AIS would not be a headline stealer, because it does not convey the same emotional emphasis as "robotics". So Robo-Advisors it is!

This chapter provides a review of what they are and what they are not: neither fully "Robots", nor truly "Advisors".

2.2 WHAT IS A ROBO-ADVISOR?

Robo-Advisors were born recently within the FinTech ecosystem to advise or manage private wealth and disintermediate traditional wealth managers. Although a truly global phenomenon, with established players in Europe and Asia-Pacific, the US is their biggest market in terms of number of players and assets under management (AUM). This is due to structural differences in the marketplaces, the US landscape being far more fragmented and competitive with a longer tradition of personal financial advisors and firms. From a timeline perspective, they first appeared between 2008 and 2010, and then made a leap onto the top chart of disruptive innovations towards 2013 due to a set of concomitant factors, among which:

- a widespread tightening of international regulations to foster investors' protection and favour *de facto* fee-only advice: for example, the European Market in Financial Instruments Directive (MiFID II), the UK Retail Distribution Review (RDR), the Australian Future of Financial Advice reform (FoFA), the FINRA and DOL rules in the US;
- a significant growth of their assets under management or under advice, favoured by a period of relative strength of US stocks;
- the impressive market penetration of smartphones, which allows a larger population of consumers to benefit from the internet any time, anywhere, than ever before;
- the recognition that Robo-Advisors do not appeal only to low margin customers of retail banking or HENRYs (High Earners, Not Rich Yet), but also to affluent and wealthier patrimonies, which were previously thought to be the *apanage* of traditional advisory firms.

Don Abbondio, one of the main characters of Alessandro Manzoni's masterpiece *The Betrothed* (1840), was a quiet clergyman. Pondering in his armchair while reading a small book, yet unaware of the disruptive events which were about to shake up his life, he found himself thinking: "*Carneades, who was he?*". Similarly, we might have been asking ourselves:

> "*Robo-Advisors, who are they?*"

A short definition cannot easily be found, because there seems to be more than one business model in the ecosystem. They differentiate by the degree of passive management, depth of investment automation, self-assessment mechanisms, and target clientele. Not all FinTechs addressing personal finance can be classified as Robo-Advisors, and not all Robo-Advisors are pure FinTechs. As a matter of fact, recognized established institutions have also launched robo-services, as add-on offers to their traditional operations. They are growing at an even faster pace than FinTech innovators. Other retail and private banks, platforms, and asset managers are following suit. Therefore, we need to articulate a rich enough definition that embraces a few of the main features of these tech based, finance-orientated firms. Although they appear to be simple solutions, there is much more complexity behind the scenes, as with anything at the crossroads between finance and technology.

> "*Robo-Advisors (1.0) are automated investment solutions which engage individuals with digital tools featuring advanced customer experience, to guide them through a self-assessment process and shape their investment behaviour towards rudimentary goal-based decision-making, conveniently supported by portfolio rebalancing techniques using trading algorithms based on passive investments and diversification strategies.*"

By extrapolating from this definition, Robo-Advisors 1.0 show at least some of these five facets, if not all:

- to be digital businesses, with automation and technology at their core;
- to conform by and large to passive investment and diversification principles;
- to institutionalize automated portfolio rebalancing and tax optimization (often);
- to use attractive self-assessment approaches which attempt to personalize investment decisions to individual goals and behaviour;
- to display a high degree of business focus.

Existing practices are just a first step in the journey of industry transformation, as further change is underway. So far, Robo-Advisors have been characterized by a strong focus on simplicity and cost efficiency compared to more advanced alternatives. Although a long-term limitation, this is also a key feature of successful innovations: simplicity usually pays off at the start of a new disruptive journey. Figure 2.1 provides a high-level example of the most common workflow of a Robo-Advisor 1.0.

On-boarding new customers seems to be one of their strengths, since they use digital experiences to reach out and facilitate intuitive self-profiling compared to

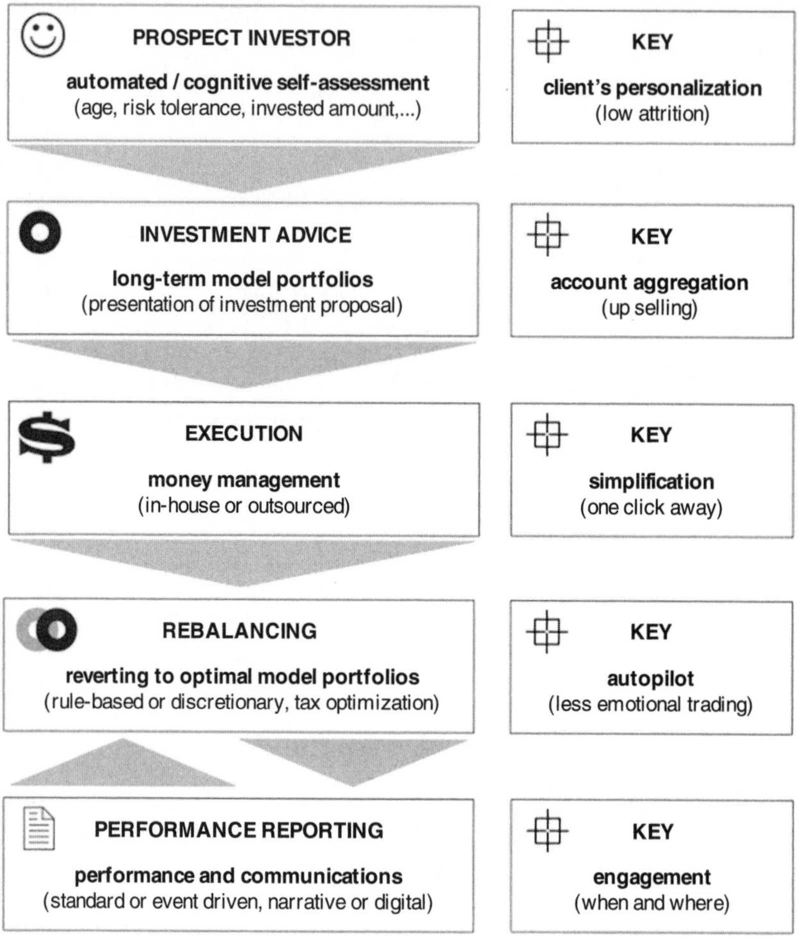

PROSPECT INVESTOR
automated / cognitive self-assessment
(age, risk tolerance, invested amount,...)

KEY
client's personalization
(low attrition)

INVESTMENT ADVICE
long-term model portfolios
(presentation of investment proposal)

KEY
account aggregation
(up selling)

EXECUTION
money management
(in-house or outsourced)

KEY
simplification
(one click away)

REBALANCING
reverting to optimal model portfolios
(rule-based or discretionary, tax optimization)

KEY
autopilot
(less emotional trading)

PERFORMANCE REPORTING
performance and communications
(standard or event driven, narrative or digital)

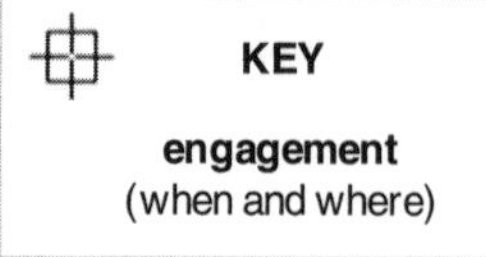

FIGURE 2.1 Robo-Advisors' automated process

paper questionnaires. Yet, we will discuss the limitations of current experiences and the need to adopt a stronger profiling mechanism to achieve a more insightful elicitation of individuals' risk tolerances and ambitions, which cognitive computing seem to facilitate. Investment advice is moving from products to model portfolios based on simple ETF strategies, attempting to lock clients into longer-term investing instead of myopic trading. This seems to be key to providing simpler investment opportunities which are linked to broader market movements instead of idiosyncratic names, reducing efforts in investment design and performance reporting. Account aggregation capabilities are also extremely valuable, if not one of the most relevant features. Individuals might not want their advisors to know about all their invested assets but they might enjoy receiving self-directed robo-advice on their full wealth allocation. The advisory workflow is improved by automating the rebalancing activities, which also partially mitigates clients' anxiety during a downturn as decision-making is delegated. Reporting becomes more interactive and visual compared to traditional reports.

The remainder of this chapter reviews the five characteristics which make up the definition of Robo-Advisors, and highlights strengths and weaknesses: digital tools, passive investments, automated rebalancing, efficient on-boarding, single minded business.

2.3 AUTOMATED DIGITAL BUSINESSES FOR UNDERSERVED MARKETS

Robo-Advisors offer financial services by leveraging on advanced digital technology, which grants scalability and enhanced customer experience to optimize clients' on-boarding and investment management. The digital transformation of everyday life is a global trend which creates the fundamental fertilizer for the success of automated investment services. This process of virtualization of the consuming experience is driven by two relevant factors: ubiquitous connectivity and generational shifts. First of all, the web has become omnipresent. The entrepreneurial exuberance of the late 1990s, which ended with the DotCom bubble, was based on too optimistic assumptions about the use and penetration of the internet. Those assumptions are realistic today: smartphones, tablets, and wearables have made digital much easier and more affordable. Second, a new generation of consumers has been growing up with total familiarity in the use of social media and digital tools. Millennials display a level of digital instincts which Baby Boomers do not possess and which makes them very receptive to FinTechs' propositions. This prompts a radical shift in behaviours. However, we can observe that digital technology is changing the consuming behaviour of all generations, not just that of young tribes.

Robo-Advisors are taking advantage of the digitalization of everyday life. They lower the barrier to entry by automating investment processes with seemingly unmanned interaction, hence minimum operating costs. Initially, they were targeting low income Millennials, thus a population with limited access to human financial advice. Given their perceived market irrelevance, this family of investors had been rather neglected by banks. *Prima facie* Robo-Advisors were meant to be a breakthrough in such an underserved (i.e., low competition from banks) but highly digitalized (i.e., sensitive to innovation) market segment. Yet, Robo-Advisors started to appeal very fast to a broader public of investors, such as affluent and high net worth individuals, who are instead at the core of incumbents' strategies. The average age, wealth, and disposable income of today's robo-clientele are all growing, highlighting that clients are segmenting themselves according to their tech-savviness instead of traditional criteria. Figure 2.2 reports on total and average AUM per

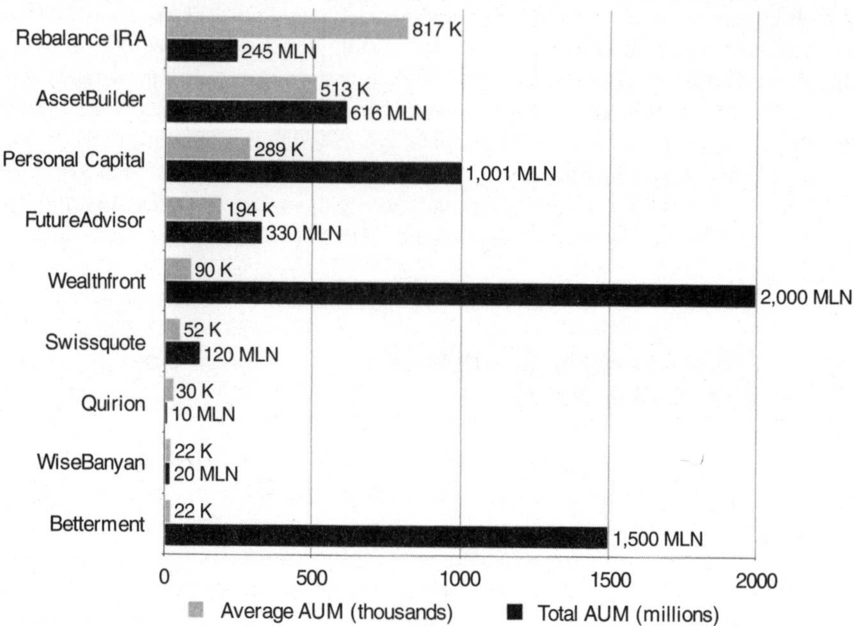

FIGURE 2.2 Robo-Advisors' AUM (US dollars)

client of a set of "independent" Robo-Advisors, as reported by MyPrivateBanking (2015).

As unexpected competition gathered in front of banking gates, incumbents' digital strategies were shaken by an earthquake, making Robo-Advisors one of the most debated topics at conferences and in the financial press.

2.4 PASSIVE INVESTMENT MANAGEMENT WITH ETFs

The second facet of Robo-Advisors is passive investment management, which is a form of trading seeking to gain or shed exposure to broader market indices, sectors, or geographies. While passive investing tracks a benchmark or a well defined subset of its components, active management attempts to achieve above market returns by trading or shorting the constituents of an index based on rules, sentiment, or portfolio managers' views. Financial literature and academic research have openly criticized the performance of active management funds compared to passive investments. Arnott, Berkin and Ye (2000) have shown that active mutual funds have underperformed the Vanguard S&P 500 index fund by an average of 2.1% per year pre-tax over a 20-year period. Their poor historical performance can be explained by a mix of factors. First, active funds ask taxable investors for higher fees, which eat up on their net returns over time. Second, they might have suffered from poor securities selection, due to a forced overweight bias towards small cap stocks compared to large ones. The investigation period (1978–1998) was dominated by large cap performances and a significantly skewed distribution of market capitalization towards large issuers: only a very tiny fraction of stocks enjoyed market capitalization above index average. Last, active trading might have triggered capital gains more often than economically advisable, leading to tax inefficiency and affecting post-tax returns of taxable investors.

The wider public of private investors might not have easy access to academic evidence, but Robo-Advisors picked up the reasoning on their behalf and heavily promoted indexing and tax optimization as key features of their offering. In the aftermath of the GFC, private investors became effectively more dubious about direct investing on Wall Street, opening up their appetite for different investment services. At the same time, market regulation started to foster higher transparency when reporting investment costs to individuals. Social media blogs caught the momentum to provide intuitive comparison of prices and historical returns across financial products, granting better education to a broader public and advocating for a change of investment behaviour. The existence of the asymmetry of information might have shielded retail banks, private banks, and asset managers from the duty to transform and do more.

Adding to their competitive stance, Robo-Advisors typically invest in ETFs instead of passive mutual funds, following tighter US regulation enforcing the ban of inducements, because they generate lower investment costs on average. Moreover, they can be traded throughout the day on open markets, which facilitates the processes of automated portfolio rebalancing and tax-loss harvesting. According to Morningstar, the average expense ration of ETFs in 2010 was 6bps, which compares with 73bps for index mutual funds, whose average tax cost has been estimated at 130bps in the period 2004–2014. While the first US mutual funds to track a market index were launched back in the 1970s, the first ETF tracking the S&P500 began trading only in 1993. Initially, SEC exemptive relief was granted only to passive ETFs providing direct or inverse exposure to specific indices, while from 2008 onwards a new family of rule based ETFs was also approved, providing a higher degree of active management to meet particular investment policies. Notwithstanding lower costs and appealing trading features, ETF shares still account for only around 12% of total net assets managed by US investment companies 20 years after they first appeared. According to the *Fact Book 2015* published by Investment Company Institute (ICI), which is the national association of US investment companies (comprising mutual funds, exchange-traded funds, closed-end funds, and unit investment trusts), the total net assets managed by US investment companies in 2014 amounted to US$ 18.2 trillion, of which US$ 15.9 trillion in mutual funds and US$ 2.0 trillion in ETFs (as can be seen in Table 2.1). Yet, in the last 10 years the net assets of ETF shares more than quintupled. This growth follows a shift in the investment practice of institutional investors, but also an increased awareness of retail investors, fee-only financial advisors, and last but not least Robo-Advisors.

TABLE 2.1 ICI Fact Book 2015 report on US investment companies

Global assets invested in MF and ETF	**US$ 33.4 trillion**
US investment company total net assets	**US$ 18.2 trillion**
- Mutual funds	US$ 15.9 trillion
- Exchange-traded funds	US$ 2.0 trillion
- Closed-end funds	US$ 289 billion
- Unit investment trusts	US$ 101 billion
US household ownership of mutual funds	
- Number of households owning MF	US$ 53.2 million
- Number of individuals owning MF	US$ 90.4 million
- % of households owning MF	43.3%
- Median MF assets of fund-owning households	US$ 103,000
- Median number of MF owned	4
US retirement market	
- Total retirement market assets	US$ 24.7 trillion
- % of households with tax-advantage retirement savings	63%
- IRA and DC plan assets invested in MF	US$ 7.3 trillion

Robo-Advisors have used ETFs to construct long-term taxable portfolios, and to achieve the following:

- compress the price tag to the minimum, dumping the market of traditional financial advice;
- commoditize automated portfolio management and rebalancing;
- make performance reporting an easier task;
- reduce compliance costs, risk management efforts, and market data expenses by working with a more efficient catalogue of investment products;
- link investors to market trends instead of individual stories to make the narrative of investment decision-making more affordable, transparent, and less emotional through the cycle.

US trading costs have also been lowering steadily, as reported by Jones (2002) in Figure 2.3. This has allowed some Robo-Advisors to offer automated portfolio indexing to their wealthier clients. Automated portfolio indexing uses algorithm trading mechanisms to replicate indices by trading on the underlying stocks directly, hence replacing mutual funds and ETFs altogether. The cost/benefit advantage seems to benefit from an improved performance of tax-loss harvesting, which is optimized by trading on individual stocks. ETF providers might also become commoditized in the not too distant future.

The main differences between ETFs and mutual funds are summarized in Table 2.2.

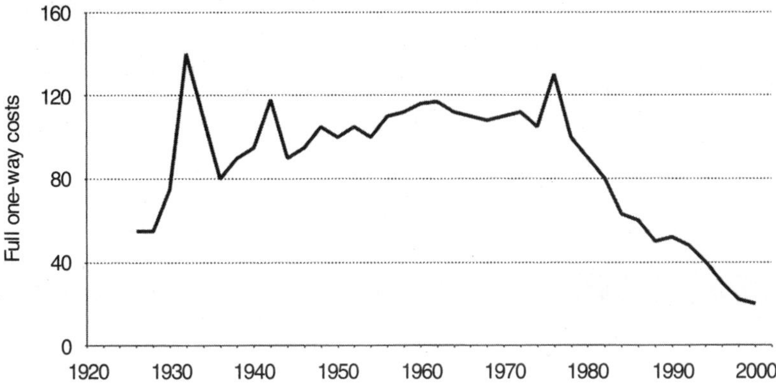

FIGURE 2.3 Average one-way trading costs on NYSE

TABLE 2.2 Main differences between ETFs and mutual funds

	ETF	Mutual Fund
Trading	Traded throughout the day.	Bought or sold directly from fund management companies at their NAV.
Transaction fees	Bid-ask spreads and brokerage commissions.	Sales loads or redemption fees.
Operation costs	Simpler and cheaper fee structure.	Articulated and less transparent fee structure.
Taxation	Tax efficient when meeting redemptions.	Tax inefficient when meeting redemptions.

2.5 ALGORITHMS OF AUTOMATED PORTFOLIO REBALANCING

Algorithms of portfolio rebalancing are the third identified facet of Robo-Advisors, and take care of the periodical revision of the asset allocation through the investment cycle. Investors are typically presented with an allocation which is chosen out of a set of pre-defined model portfolios according to a self-assessment procedure that judges on their age, risk tolerance, return appetite, financial knowledge, initial or periodic invested amount, and time horizons. Therefore, effective personalization is fairly limited even though some Robo-Advisors feature more refined thematics or allow the inclusion of personal market opinions within optimization routines. Portfolio modelling often refers to Mean-Variance or tilted optimizations (Black-Litterman), which allow the embedding of subjective views of expected returns or their relative difference across investments. The most common asset classes are stocks, bonds, currencies, commodities, and protection against inflation. In essence, rebalancing is a risk management technique which enforces the asset allocation to revert back towards its desired long-term equilibrium, because market dynamics might lead invested portfolios to deviate. Running a new mathematical optimization at every rebalancing time is not strictly required, but is recommended if markets have drifted significantly from their initial state. Existing Robo-Advisors exhibit different rebalancing rules, which are not always part of a fully automated process:

- discrete schedules (e.g., once a month);
- discretional decisions of fund managers (e.g., personal views on single asset classes);
- statistical triggers to avoid unnecessary trading and minimize costs (e.g., widening of tracking error volatility against a benchmark);
- reoptimization as new asset classes are made available or the economic environment changes abruptly (e.g., a market crash or a fundamental shift in monetary policy).

Their typical long-term and automatically rebalanced model portfolios are an attempt to keep clients invested through the market cycle, in the belief that the choices of asset allocation dominate portfolio returns in the long run. Clearly, this assumption is aligned with their revenue model, often based on fee-only agreements as a percentage of AUM. Although rebalancing is meant to facilitate the risk management of model portfolios, we must acknowledge that these are constructed with fairly simplistic or straightforward optimization routines, whose limitations are discussed in the second part of this book. Yet, are incumbents doing any better?

2.6 PERSONALIZED DECISION-MAKING, INDIVIDUAL GOALS, AND BEHAVIOUR

The fourth facet is the personalization of the investment experience across individual goals and personality. This is possibly the most compelling but challenging feature, which has been attracting a substantial amount of investment in research and development, not just from rampant technology providers but also from incumbents. Creating a truly disruptive and emotional dialogue between investors and digital firms would be the tipping point of industry robotization. As already depicted in Figure 2.1, the first and most recognized element of interaction between prospects and Robo-Advisors resides in their on-boarding mechanisms. While conventional wealth managers largely rely upon paper questionnaires to document individual investors' traits, Robo-Advisors take advantage of digital technology to shape the process of enrolment with enhanced customer experience. Today's Robo-Advisors certainly emerge as lighter engagement devices, but they are clearly not free from red tape either. Market regulation imposes that investors' risk profiles are to be properly elicited and kept up to date, although no specific approach nor criterion is defined to validate their robustness. Most configurations start from the assumption that investors are rational, inherently risk averse, and accept more risk only if they can garner higher expected returns to compensate for it. Therefore, the key difference compared to conventional wealth managers does not seem to reside so much in the underlying assumptions but rather in a more attractive process, which makes questionnaires look less so and enhances the perception of investors' participation in the decision-making process. The model portfolio identified at the end of the self-assessment should be perceived by investors as a more logical choice of their own opinions, instead of a third party's recommendation: given their age, their capability to absorb losses and their declared return ambitions. The delicacies of the processes dedicated to risk profiling are an unresolved problem both in practice as well as in academia, irrespective of the level of automation. Hence, this should be a top priority for wealth management firms, Robo-Advisors included: only a consistent and transparent elicitation of individual goals and fears is a guarantee that the subsequent steps of automated investing are truly robust and suitable. Moreover, only a thorough and informative process can open up to further advances in personal finance, like consistent Goal Based Investing. Should Robo-Advisors provide only a better experience, but then rely on the same principles of conventional questionnaires, they might improve the framework but not solve the problem. Recent seminal papers have discussed the inability of conventional questionnaires to elicit investors' attitudes and behaviour with regard to risk-taking. Kahneman and Tversky (1979), Foerster, Linnainmaa, Melzer and Prebevitero (2014), Burns and Slovic (2012), Weber, Weber and Nosic (2012), and Klement (2015) are all valid references and will be discussed more thoroughly in the second part of this book, which is dedicated to investors, risk profiling and advanced technology to better account for behavioural finance, the framing bias, the evidence stemming from the biology of risk, and the variability of risk feelings. Table 2.3 provides a summary of the strengths and weaknesses of Robo-Advisors, compared to conventional wealth managers, with respect to self-assessment and enrolling tasks.

2.7 SINGLE MINDED BUSINESSES

The last common feature of Robo-Advisors resides in their highly focused propositions, which attempt to unbundle one aspect at the time of the banking experience. Such single mindedness is clearly a strength in the short term, as disruptive innovation has a chance to succeed only if consumers can understand the new

TABLE 2.3 Self-assessment and enrolment: strengths and weaknesses

Strengths	Weaknesses
Improved customer experience.	Rather "one size fits all", do not account for truly idiosyncratic needs.
Investment goals represented graphically, facilitated coherent articulation of personal ambitions.	Individuals have multiple goals, need of assistance to filter them.
Higher empowerment in the initial decision-making process, can shape investment behaviour thereafter.	Too much reliance on capability to self-assign a risk aversion, cannot judge if ready to invest or need time to think (e.g., talk to spouse).

offer without ambiguity, are granted easy access to the new product, recognize the differences compared to conventional providers, and feel they can afford it. Moreover, simple front ends allow Robo-Advisors to be primarily and *de facto* very efficient enrolling mechanisms, to reduce the attrition rate during the steps of self-assessment and minimize the percentage of customers who drop out before signing up their commitment to invest. These aspects might not be the only ones to play in favour of their single mindedness. Robo-Advisors are still fairly indebted companies, they need to grow fast and reward venture capital investments. This might further reinforce their need to push aggressively on their original message and exploit the current momentum of favourable coverage by the press and social media. Notwithstanding, the landscape is changing fast and will change even faster in the next years. On-boarding new customers is not cost free and requires significant marketing expenditures to augment AUM from the first billion to the first trillion, and fully exploit digital economies of scale. As the cost to acquire a new client is fairly insensitive to a client's disposable wealth (at least when looking at customers of retail banking and affluent investors), Robo-Advisors might feel the pressure to reach out to individuals outside their original retail focus. Yet, the greater the amount of wealth invested by an individual, the more likely the request for extra added value compared to current configurations, inducing them to articulate a broader offer, such as opening to other investment options or a more refined identification of personal goals. The following set of elements concur to transform existing AIS into Robo-Advisors 2.0:

- competition from established institutions, which are starting to adopt robo-technology as standalone products or to support the work of human financial advisors, potentially reducing the clients' perception of the gap between fully automated solutions and hybrid business models;

- pressure from institutional investors to improve their return on investment, by increasing the profitability per customer;
- opportunity to optimize marketing costs, and appeal to wealthier individuals.

Robo-Advisors 2.0 might therefore expand their initial propositions and feature some of the following characteristics:

- transform from Business to Consumer models (B2C) into Business to Business to Consumer services (B2B2C) or Robo-4-Advisors, and provide personal financial advisors with the opportunity to use robo-technology for those parts of their workflow related to account aggregation, model portfolio selection, rebalancing, and reporting;
- in some cases, transform to Business to Business models (B2B) or Robo-as-a-Service, and provide On Cloud services to Tier 2 financial institutions looking for automation but lacking the expertise to develop proprietary solutions;
- extend the services offered towards a better definition of personal goals along the time axis, hence fostering convergence between financial advice and planning;
- expand into saving and payment platforms, not just investment solutions;
- augment the effective personalization of model portfolios, and account more explicitly for the opinions of more sophisticated investors or demanding financial advisors;
- transform into fully fledged digital family offices, adding specialized services of wealth optimization beyond financial investments;
- engage clients with Gamification to further align their investment behaviour to long-term money management, solve the educational burden, and sell more complex and higher margin services which would otherwise require human interaction.

Clearly, unbundling financial services and focusing on one aspect of the banking relationship in isolation might be a good starting point for a FinTech, but not necessarily a proper long-term strategy for an institution. Banks are well aware of the relevance of creating a marketplace, where wealth management is an essential entry point to create a banking relationship that facilitates cross-selling: loans, mortgages, and insurance products.

2.8 PRINCIPLES OF TAX-LOSS HARVESTING

Robo-Advisors have been positioning aggressively to provide above average returns compared to passive investments managed by conventional financial advisors. Above average returns are meant to come from a potentially superior performance of long-term asset allocations which do not attempt to tame the markets, as well as methodical attention to expense ratios by minimizing management fees, trading costs, and tax implications. They attempt to generate slightly better returns by enriching rebalancing algorithms with tax-saving mechanisms that optimize tax liabilities (after-tax benefits) and reinvest tax savings for longer periods (before-tax advantages). This seems to be particularly relevant in those constituencies like the US in which the tax code allows taxable investors to take advantage of losses generated by declined investments, which are disposed of to harness tax reductions and lower personal taxes.

Tax-loss harvesting does not provide tax avoidance, but is a tax-deferral mechanism which exploits the different tax treatment between short and long term. Most of all, it combines the need to respect the asset allocation constraints at any point in time with the restrictions of the tax code (e.g., wash sale rules). These algorithms search for declined investments to generate losses, provide tax reductions, lower an investor's taxes, and minimize the negative impact of wash sales, which disallows a loss if taxable investors do not truly dispose of the investment across all their accounts (e.g., accounts held by their spouses). With regard to the US tax code, the rule would be triggered by selling a security and purchasing a "substantially identical" security 30 days before or after the sale. Since Robo-Advisors cannot freely dispose of declined losses, they typically replace declined assets with correlated ones, that is assets which are not "substantially identical" for the tax code but whose returns are highly correlated to the original ones from a portfolio management perspective. That could be the case for ETFs which provide the same market exposure but formally track different market indices (e.g., MSCI Emerging Markets versus FTSE Emerging Markets). Investment catalogues are therefore made up of primary and secondary lists, which the algorithms can choose from. The use of correlated securities allows us to maintain the target asset allocation and optimize the cash drag that would be generated by the application of wash sale rules. When harvesting losses without replacement, wealth managers are exposed to the risk that within the 30-day period the potential tax losses stemming from a decline in the security are more than offset by a reversal of the security's price in the open market, which will end up generating a capital gain and leave the investor worse off if the resulting gains exceed the harvested losses. The use of the correlated asset instead, allows harvesting of further losses if after 30 days the security's price has further declined, or generated portfolio performance without triggering any capital gain if the security price has gone up since no further buy/sell is required.

Hence, tax-loss harvesting attempts to generate so-called TaxAlpha advantages, which can be attributed to the reinvestment of tax savings and the difference in the tax rate between short and long term. The benefits of tax-loss harvesting clearly disappear when a portfolio is liquidated and taxes are finally due, as long as the portfolio is not passed on to the investor's heirs or a charity fund. Since TaxAlpha measurement is exposed to the uncertainty of liquidation, it is typically computed yearly, the year being the time frame under which taxes are fully due and investment losses can offset other capital gains or income taxes.

$$\text{TaxAlpha} = \frac{CL_{ST}X_{ST} + CL_{LT}X_{LT}}{V_{PORT}} \tag{2.1}$$

where CL_{ST} is the short-term capital loss, CL_{LT} is the long-term capital loss, and X_{ST} and X_{LT} are the corresponding short-term and long-term federal and state capital gains tax rates.

Portfolio rebalancing is performed at least once a month and taxable gains and liabilities can be automatically assessed with regard to the characteristics of individual investors. Therefore, automated robo-technology allows FinTechs to save time and achieve economies of scale beyond the capabilities of most conventional financial advisors. In general, not all investors can benefit. First of all, only long-term investors can be advantaged since tax codes usually impose higher taxes to short-term compared to longer-term capital gains. Second, wealthier investors bearing higher tax rate obligations or living in higher tax rate constituencies have more to gain than those falling into lower tax brackets. The differences in tax code among countries are not discussed in this book and the presentation of tax optimization techniques is kept to the level of principles. The following example is only indicative and does not necessarily correspond to any practice.

Example

Frank is our investor. He lives in a zero cost trading environment and falls into a tax bracket which imposes 25% on short-term capital gains and 15% on long-term capital gains. The financial market is made up of three different opportunities:

- ETF_A tracking the FTSE US Index;
- ETF_{B1} tracking the MSCI Emerging Markets Index;
- ETF_{B2} tracking the FTSE Emerging Markets Index.

ETF_{B1} and ETF_{B2} are known to be perfectly correlated (to simplify our example), but are not "substantially identical" according to the tax code. Frank has US$ 200,000 sitting in his account and wants to invest half of his money with a short investment horizon (i.e., 1 year) and the remaining half with a longer horizon (i.e., 5 years). Therefore, he makes the following investment decision at the beginning of the first year:

- invest US$ 100,000 into ETF_A for 1 year;
- invest US$ 100,000 into ETF_{B1} for 5 years.

Frank is committed to his investment style. Thus, he plans to disinvest from ETF_A at the end of the first year and disinvest from ETF_{B1} at the end of the fifth year.

TABLE 2.4 ETFs US$ value over time

Time	T_0	T_1	T_2	T_3	T_4	T_5
ETF_A	100,000	107,000	-	-	-	-
ETF_{B1}	100,000	93,000	97,000	103,000	115,000	130,000
ETF_{B2}	100,000	93,000	97,000	103,000	115,000	130,000

Table 2.4 shows the evolution of the market value of the three investments over time.

As planned, Frank disposes of ETF_A at T_1 and incurs a short-term capital gain equal to US$ 7,000, which will be taxed at 25%. Frank now has two options:

1. pay taxes on his short-term capital at T_1 and carry on with his investment in ETF_{B1} until T_5, leading up to a long-term capital gain of US$ 30,000 taxable at 15%;
2. optimize his taxes by disposing of ETF_{B1} at T_1, harvesting a tax-loss of US$ 7,000 to offset the capital gains generated by ETF_A and immediately reinvest the proceeds of ETF_{B1} into ETF_{B2}, which is then kept in the portfolio until T_5 to yield a long-term capital gain equal to US$ 37,000 taxable at 15%.

We can easily see that:

1. in the first case, Frank pays taxes of US$ 1,750 at T_1 and taxes of US$ 4,500 at T_5;
2. in the second case, Frank compensates short-term capital gains and losses at T_1 and defers taxation until T_5 of an amount equal to US$ 5,550.

2.9 CONCLUSIONS

Robo-Advisors are automated investment solutions which have been showcasing how digital technology, automated investment algorithms, and passive investment management can be bundled together to transform the functioning of the wealth management industry. Born to serve the needs of taxable investors directly, they are already transforming into Business to Business models to support the work of personal financial advisors and planners. The personalization of the investment decision-making experience around personal goals and fears is part of their success story, and configures as a very rudimentary implementation of Goal Based Investing principles. Finally, the strengths and weaknesses of Robo-Advisors 1.0 can be summarized as in Table 2.5.

TABLE 2.5 Digital technology: strengths and weaknesses

Strengths	Weaknesses
Advanced technology, no dependency on obsolete legacy systems.	Budget restriction to access further technology advancements.
ETFs minimize trading costs, investment processes institutionalized on compact product catalogue.	Reliance to passive management could be a limiting factor to service broader and wealthier clientele.
Investment decisions less emotional with automated rebalancing.	Still to demonstrate AUM retention during severe market downturns.
Sense of personal empowerment, perceived personalization of goals and timeline.	Model portfolios not truly tailored.
Efficient on-boarding mechanisms with high degree of business focus.	Not easy to transform into the next generation and provide higher margin services.

The next chapter discusses the functioning of the investment management industry and how robo-technology is poised to change the competitive landscape of the supply-demand chain: asset managers, ETF providers, platforms, personal financial advisors, retail and private banks.

CHAPTER 3

The Transformation of the Supply-Side

"Silicon Valley is coming."

—James Dimon (1956–)

The supply-demand chain of the investment management industry connects the offer-side to the demand-side of the wealth management game. The functioning of this highly regulated business requires the interaction of a variety of professional players, among which active and passive fund managers, ETF providers, platforms, discount brokers, retail and private banks, personal financial advisors, and Robo-Advisors. Roles, incentives, and modality of interaction are described, to highlight their critical challenges in today's digital world. Discerning how intermediaries make money is essential to learn how to make best use of technology and innovation to dispute or transform their business models.

3.1 INTRODUCTION

Banking, including investment management, facilitates many aspects of commerce and trade, the funding of governments and corporations, the financing of personal needs, and the settlement of all payments. Investment management relates to the origination, structuring, and management of financial assets. Personal wealth, owned by the richest few or the millions of retail bank customers is globally worth hundreds of trillions of US$ equivalent assets and contributes to most of its income. The industry targets to make profits by linking the offer-side to the demand-side: issuers of financial products (governments, financial institutions, or corporations) can access modern financial markets and meet the saving and investment demand of institutional and private investors. The supply-demand mechanisms are not straightforward but investors and issuers are typically intermediated by professional players: asset managers, investment banks, platforms, and wealth managers. In this game of finance, issuers search for the cheapest funding, investors look for the highest risk-adjusted return, and intermediaries make use of their professional knowledge to serve their clients and maximize intermediation margins. Conflicts of interest can easily arise as financial conglomerates often embrace a vast amount of services, which are directed to both issuers and investors. Therefore, banking and market regulation has been put in place to rein in the behaviour of all professional players, and safeguard the interests of final investors. Yet, the industry is not free from scandals. Greed and investment exuberance have often facilitated the building of large imbalances, which have grown into bubbles and burst into market downturns and painful recessions of real economies. Currently, the whole industry is hit by a perfect storm: while post-crisis regulation is threatening the main mechanisms of profit sharing among the players (e.g., the ban on retrocessions), social media and the internet are changing the behaviour of modern investors (e.g., acceptance of non-conventional investment services, any time, anywhere) and digital technology is facilitating the rise of disruptive entrants. The principles of innovation theory and the main characteristics of Robo-Advisors have been discussed. We can proceed to review the functioning of the industry in broader terms, and highlight how robo-technology can transform traditional wealth management relationships and the way taxable investors trade financial securities. This is of the utmost relevance, since the industry is struggling to move out of a product-orientated distribution framework and centre more on client/portfolio advice.

3.2 THE INVESTMENT MANAGEMENT SUPPLY-DEMAND CHAIN

The origins of the industry can be traced back to the Italian Renaissance, when banks thrived to serve the needs of wealthy families. Yet, only in the 20th century has investment management become a mass market industry, appealing to both customers of retail banking and ultra high net worth individuals. This became particularly evident in the 1950s, which saw the ranks of the middle class soaring in numbers and worth. The industry has transformed significantly ever since, particularly due to technology advances which have enabled the automation of back office processes and security trading. However, investment decision-making has been characterized by a conventional model, in which private investors have been largely assisted by human advisors or brokers. Yet, a process of progressive commoditization has been slowly eroding the dominant position of once established intermediaries, as presented in Figure 3.1. Discount brokers made financial advice accessible to the US middle class and have acquired a large portion of AUM since their appearance in the 1970s. Online trading was made available to an even larger public of self-directed investors

50s CONVENTIONAL ADVISORS
HNW - UHNW
(human dialogue, high advisory price)

70s DISCOUNT BROKERS
Affluent - Retail
(human dialogue, medium advisory price)

90s ONLINE TRADING
Mainly Affluent and Retail
(limited human dialogue, low transaction price)

now ROBO-ADVISORS
Mainly Retail - adding tiers
(usually no human dialogue, low advisory price)

FIGURE 3.1 Investment management industry

in the 1990s, although in truth confined to a specialized group of trading-orientated individuals. Nowadays, Robo-Advisors seem to possess the potential to achieve what discount brokers did forty years ago and further downshift the costs and complexities of the investment experience.

The industry supply-demand chain is organized along three main branches: issuers (primary and secondary), intermediaries, and final investors (as in Figure 3.2). Business reality is more varied and features many more interdependencies. We can distinguish between issuers of direct and indirect investments. The first are issuers of debt and capital claims (bonds and stocks) which, helped by investment banks, fulfil their financing needs or meet their risk-management requirements. The second allow investors and their intermediaries to efficiently gain indirect exposure to the risk-return profiles of primary securities. Intermediaries are asset managers and wealth managers which serve final investors and advise them on suitable products or portfolios, by selecting among direct or indirect investments. Platforms allow

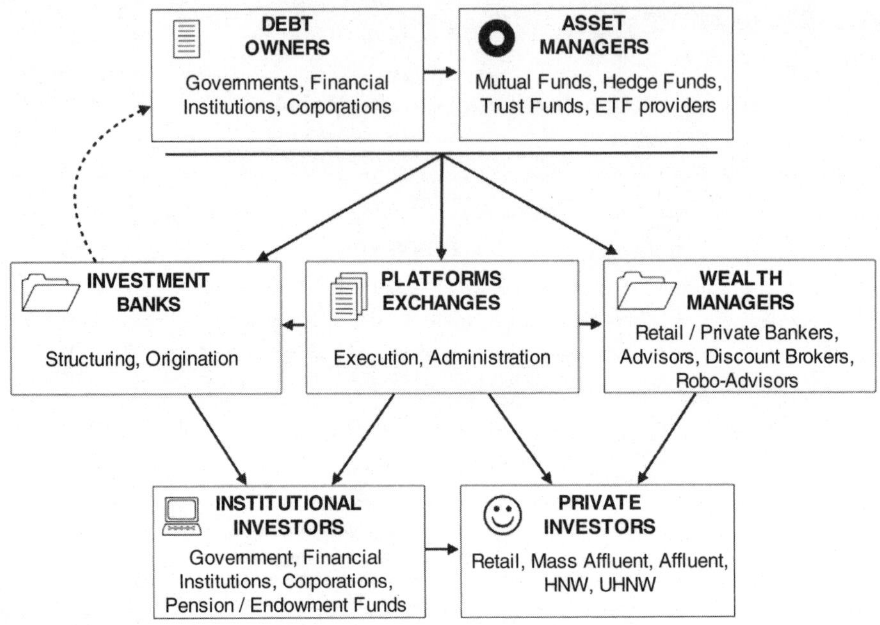

FIGURE 3.2 Investment management industry

intermediaries and final investors to trade securities within organized and transparent frameworks. Final investors can either be institutions (e.g., pension funds) or taxable investors (e.g., individuals), looking for yield and financial advice.

What follows is a presentation of the characteristics of these actors and some of the products they sell, and a discussion of the threats that they face due to progressive digitalization and robo-advice.

3.3 HOW INTERMEDIARIES MAKE MONEY

The essence of investment management is to connect issuers and investors through distribution channels, and allow the latter to buy/sell financial securities to achieve their personal goals. Clearly, the change of approach from a product-centric to a client/portfolio-centric model can only be successful if the incentive schemes that regulate the behaviour of individual wealth managers to place financial securities in clients' portfolios are aligned. A financial instrument is a contract representing the right to receive future benefits under a stated set of conditions. Taxable investors can build direct exposure into any different type of claim on a financial, corporate, or government entity (e.g., bond). Alternatively, they can hold exposures through

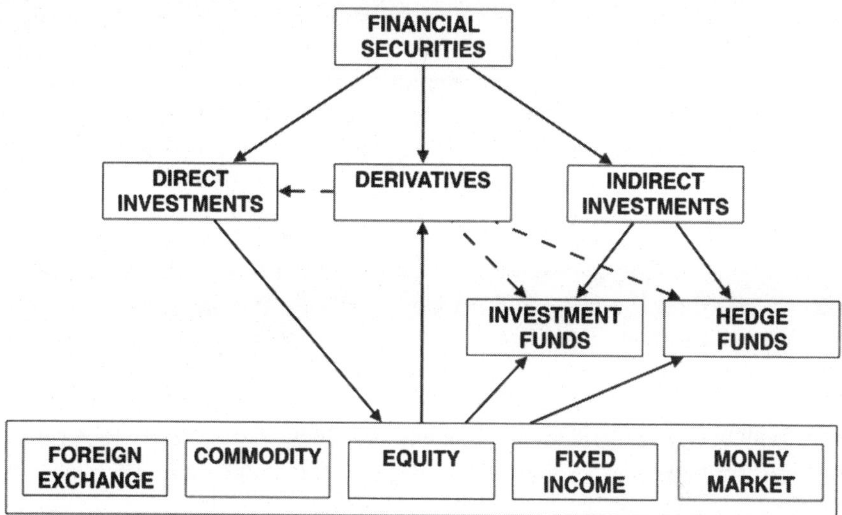

FIGURE 3.3 Financial securities

investment vehicles (e.g., mutual fund) that offer quotes in the portfolio of financial instruments they hold. Bonds, stocks, mutual funds, ETFs, structured notes, and certificates are all securities. Hedge funds are not offered to a broader retail public but only to wealthy individuals, while listed derivatives are negotiated by investors which are more trading-orientated. The hierarchy in Figure 3.3 represents a common way of classifying financial securities. Direct investments are straight claims on a financial, corporate, or government entity such as bonds and equities. Indirect investments are indirect claims on a financial, corporate, or government such as shares of investment funds. Derivatives are indirect claims on the performance of financial, corporate, or government-related securities, so that the investor receives or pays out according to a formula linked to the appreciation/depreciation of an underlying financial element which is itself a direct investment (e.g., an equity), an indirect investment (e.g., an investment fund), or an index.

Intermediaries have built powerful distribution channels to place these financial products in the pockets of the broader public, learning to make money according to four major schemes:

- **Commission only:** they receive commissions for selling financial products to investors. Such commissions can be directly requested of investors or are embedded in the financial transaction. For example, embedded fees in structured products or retrocessions from asset managers.
- **Commission and fee:** they collect commissions for selling products to investors, but also ask for fees to provide investment planning assistance.

- **Salary and bonus:** investment professionals working for financial institutions (e.g., discount brokers or retail banks) get higher compensation for recommending or selling certain products and services.
- **Fee-only:** personal financial advisors (e.g., Registered Investment Advisors in the US) are paid by investors for their advice on ongoing investment management. They must have no financial stake in what they recommend.

Fees can be flat, performance-related, or a mix of the two. Performance fees might seem to incentivize wealth managers to do more, select better products, and provide better advice to their customers. However, they could also induce advisors to leverage too much risk on behalf of their customers, in an attempt to enhance the chances to harvest higher margins, especially in a downturn. Flat fees could instead induce advisors to do the minimum required and walk away, although they might facilitate a better alignment of the investment policies for more conservative individuals. A mix of the two, thus a waterfall model based on a flat floor and some participation in excess performance, might reconcile this dichotomy.

So far, the most common incentive plan has been the "commission and fee", since institutions host more than one distribution model and intermediate a broad range of direct and indirect securities. Therefore, commissions and retrocessions have been traditionally harnessed as a percentage of private money traded or invested: a few basis points for stocks, more than one hundred for actively managed investment funds. With recent changes in market regulation, prompting the banning of retrocessions or fostering higher transparency on costs, this revenue model has been subjected to stress vis-á-vis more independent "fee-only" approaches. Clearly, this would be a Copernican revolution of the incentive skeleton of most financial institutions.

3.4 ISSUERS OF DIRECT CLAIMS (DEBT OWNERS)

Bonds and equities are the building blocks of most investment opportunities: they are issued by debt owners and final investors can trade them directly or as part of investment funds. The main buyers are financial institutions (investment banks and insurance companies) and fund managers (pension funds and mutual funds). Although bonds and equities remain a very large component of private investors' portfolios, evidence shows that US households have already come to progressively favour investment funds, particularly in the aftermath of the GFC and following the growth of Individual Retirement Accounts (IRA) and Defined Contribution (DC) plans. Hence, their demand for directly held equities and bonds has started to fall, as can be seen in Figure 3.4 (source *Investment Company Fact Book 2015*). Yet, the global demand for bonds and equities has increased steadily together with the growth of global wealth, net of market fluctuations. Recently, this expansion has been fostered by a series of factors related to lower than average interest rates in major economies and stronger than ever demand in growth markets.

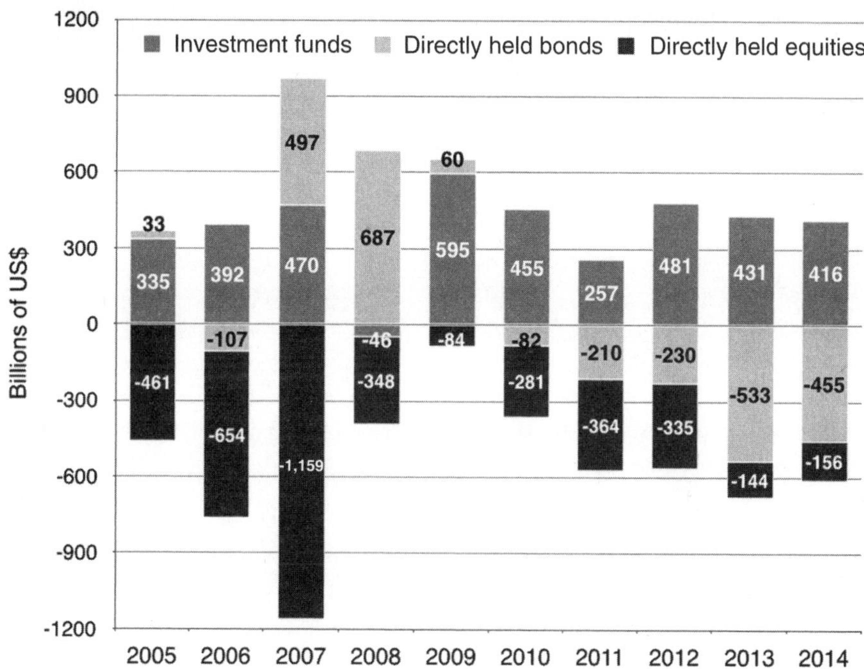

FIGURE 3.4 Households net investments in funds, bonds, and equities (US 2005–2014)

Table 3.1 reports the size of global debt and capital markets in US$ equivalents.

Recent behaviour of private investors in relying more on investment funds is a relevant shift for the wealth management industry, particularly for commercial banks. They might expect to report a reduction in commercial margins stemming from bond origination and underwriting and an increase in the relevance of investment funds. This trend seems to be a consequence of two factors. First, investors' reaction to the GFC, which has scared them, lowering their appetite for direct participation in debt and capital markets. Second, increasing investors' perception of the value of passive investments, which come with easier to achieve benefits of portfolio diversification. This shift seems to favour the acceptance of single minded Robo-Advisors' propositions.

3.5 THE INSTITUTIONALIZATION OF THE PRIVATE BANKING RELATIONSHIP

Private and retail banks play a central role in the wealth management relationship, and their distribution channels allocate the largest amount of AUM towards direct and indirect investment vehicles worldwide. Private banking primarily refers to the

TABLE 3.1 Debt and equity markets (US$ trillions)

Year	Debt Securities*	Equity Markets**
2000	5.4	30.9
2001	6.3	26.5
2002	7.7	22.8
2003	9.7	20.6
2004	11.5	36.8
2005	11.9	40.9
2006	15.0	50.7
2007	18.4	60.9
2008	18.9	32.6
2009	20.9	47.8
2010	20.9	55.0
2011	21.0	47.2
2012	21.9	54.7
2013	22.8	64.1
2014	21.9	67.8

*Notional of international issues (data from Bank of International Settlement).
**Capitalization of domestic markets (data from World Exchange Federation).

managing of patrimonies of wealthy individuals (e.g., investments and financial planning, securities, and real assets) whose known disposable wealth is typically more than US$ 1 million equivalent. Clearly, this is not a binding threshold and institutions apply a different tiering according to internal policy or market conditions (e.g., Eastern European banks set the entry point lower than their core Europe counterparts). Yet, the US$ 1 million cut is commonly used by market analysts to tell HNW and UHNW apart. Retail banking instead provides more off-the-shelf commercial services (e.g., investments, mortgages, loans, payments) and can feature more easily a combination of human types of relationship management (e.g., branches, call centres, branded financial advisors) and internet engagement (self-directed online banking). Seemingly, private and retail banks provide overlapping services (e.g., investments) but deliver them with very different content and format (e.g., buy and sell versus wealth planning), as private banking tends to be more personalized and human intensive so that only wealthy individuals can afford it. Their value proposition needs to stand out clearly in front of their target clientele. Therefore, private banks feature dedicated branding, processes, policies, and operations even when part of larger commercial banking groups.

Rising costs of compliance, higher transparency in the disclaimers of costs faced by taxable investors, if not banning of the retrocessions between intermediaries and asset managers (e.g., fiduciary standards in the US) are forcing banks to rethink the foundations of retail and private banking investment relationships. Moreover, cooperation and greater openness among international tax authorities have levelled up the playing field in favour of on-shore investments, making off-shore tax advantages much less attractive if not unfeasible and have affected private banking advantages. This has reinforced the call to increase the effective added value of their offers, to retain AUM and better engage existing clientele. Customer engagement and experience have become the mantra in all industry talks, and have reinforced the strategic importance of the digital agenda. Digital technology is indispensable to achieve enough economy of scale in fast growing environments and penetrate new markets, characterized by different client behaviour and less branding legacy compared to mature economies. The fact is that existing business models might not allow the efficient servicing of clients, particularly mass affluent and affluent segments which cannot access private banking services but might be willing to engage in further investments should this become attractive and inexpensive. The upcoming retirement crisis is also fostering an increasing need for mass market financial advice and planning, since a large cohort of Baby Boomers is about to retire in the next decade and will take care of seemingly insufficient pension contributions sponsored by governments. Underserved mass affluent and affluent individuals represent 57.5% of world wealth, as indicated in the Credit Suisse (2012) wealth pyramid featured in Figure 3.5, which also shows that 7.5% of the world's population owns *per capita* between US$ 100,000 and US$ 1 million, which accounts for 43.1% of global wealth.

The institutionalization of the private banking relationship corresponds to the need to streamline operations and extend added-value services to affluent clients. It cannot be achieved without digital investments and automated money management. While banks have started to engage in a slow process of repositioning of their offers, the increasing use of the internet and smartphones has empowered individuals to disengage from traditional banking, segmenting themselves according to their tech-savviness, knowledge, and confidence. This has facilitated the penetration of Robo-Advisors in the upper tiers of the wealth pyramid, threatening the business model of established institutions and the incentive schemes behind them, creating internal political frictions about who should service whom and how. The process of institutionalization of the wealth management relationship is mainly driven by the following factors:

- **On-shore versus off-shore:** lack of tax advantages forces a reallocation of money from off-shore to on-shore accounts, and requires the provision of better services to justify existing fees.
- **Market regulation:** higher transparency on costs and sales incentives requires a broadening of the value proposition and clearer discussion of asset allocations and personal goals, instead of individual products, highlighting an educational gap in banks' personnel and need for intuitive portfolio management tools.
- **Asian tigers:** economic growth in Asia has opened up opportunities for local and international banks, which need to adopt automated tools and digital solutions to tackle the challenges of a different and fast emerging clientele.

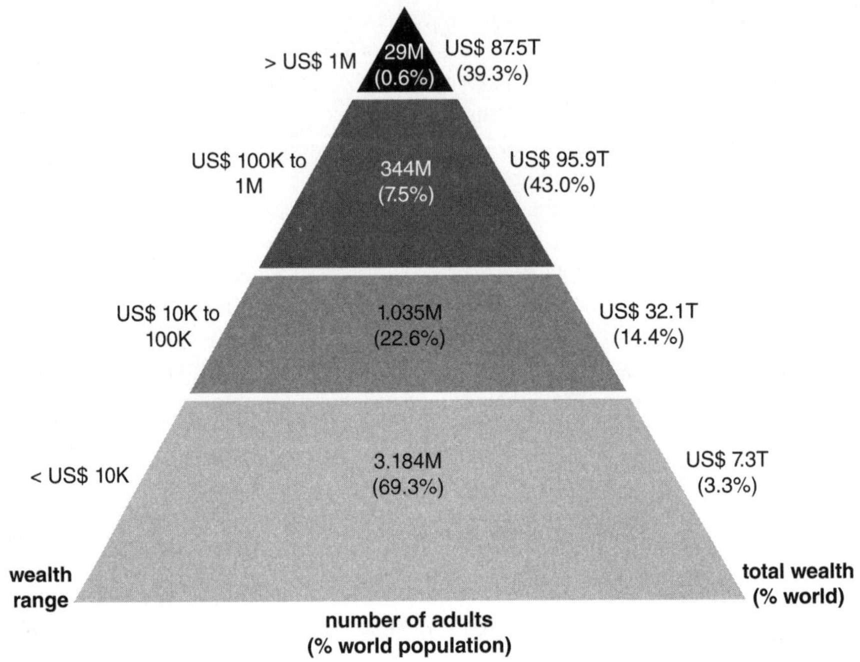

FIGURE 3.5 Households net investments in funds, bonds, and equities (US 2005–2014)

- **Independent advice:** personal financial advisors have challenged banking ownership of client relationships (particularly in the US), as they can close the knowledge gap with final investors.
- **Generational transfer:** wealth is changing hands towards younger generations that are more digital-sensitive and less loyal to established brands.
- **Robo-Advisors:** the rise of automated investment solutions has helped investors to gain more confidence in judging the intrinsic value of traditional banking services.

Financial institutions need to transform, but existing incentive models seem to create a divide between the interest of internal stakeholders and that of their clients. "Changing the bank" is an expensive process, and has been attempted a few times in recent decades but with very different focus compared to today's revolution, which sees competition rising from outside the banking club. Traditional approaches have previously operated according to two principles aimed at enhancing operational efficiency: functional excellence and the uniqueness of resources. Functional excellence corresponds to the belief that efficient firms would generate value for both customers and shareholders (such as faster origination processes, bundling of services into

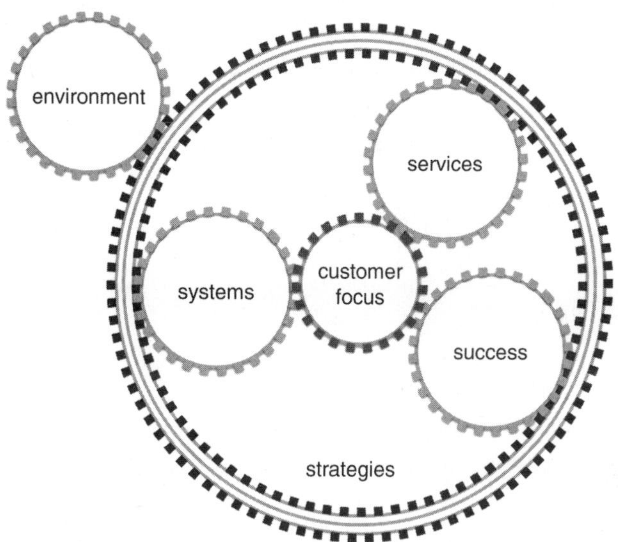

FIGURE 3.6 The Customer Value in Financial Services engine

one-stop shops, and new distribution channels like online offers). Yet, customers could not truly differentiate among these improvements which didn't necessarily result in lower costs or distinct features among competitors, as most of them could be imitated. Uniqueness of resources has been identified as a competitive hedge (e.g., a portfolio of better customers, broader risk diversification on balance sheets, access to more information, or richness of the product catalogues). Once more, customers could not truly appreciate and reward larger banks' capability to step into many different services, compared to local and smaller providers. Finally, the focus started to shift towards the customers themselves to anticipate, discern, and respond to their needs in a way that could be unique and difficult to imitate. This would move the emphasis from internal efficiency toward front-end design and building of customer-focus processes. Melnick, Nayyar, Pinedo and Seshadri (2000) have described this trend in detail and explained that value creation is the result of a smoothly running engine called Customer Value in Financial Services (CVFS), which is shown in Figure 3.6 as in their original publication. The CVFS engine has four key endogenous elements that must be carefully designed by banks to create customer focused value, and which this book discusses in the light of digitalization and robo-technology: strategies, services, systems, and measure of success. While strategies allow the shaping of the most appropriate services and aim to facilitate the best interaction between back-end legacy systems and front-end reporting tools, we can identify two other external factors which are not under the control of banks' management but interact with financial firms: customer behaviour and the broader environment.

The current strategic shift in financial markets post GFC is grounded on the search for advanced client/portfolio-orientated approaches to rebuild trust in the banking relationship. However, the recent transformational focus is not about design of client-orientated processes only, but rather taking clients' behaviour to centre stage of the supply-demand mechanism in terms of understanding their fears and ambitions and enhancing their experience and engagement. Therefore, the original exogenous and endogenous factors described in the CVFS engine can be enriched with respect to today's disruption, social mega trends, and the rise of behavioural analytics.

Exogenous factors:

- **Customer behaviour:** private investors' tastes and behaviour are transforming fast. This is particularly evident for younger generations, although wealthier Baby Boomers are also getting more engaged with digital. Peer-to-peer recommendations are becoming progressively more important. The retirement crisis, which is surfacing in mature economies, is requiring taxable investors to search for a breed of financial advice and financial planning to face the difficulties of long-term investments against personal goals.
- **Environment:** the globalization of international trade, growing interdependence among economies, and the consequences of the GFC have forced individuals, regulators, and tax authorities to tear down the barriers between on-shore and off-shore markets, with the aim of repatriating patrimonies or optimizing depleted public finances. Transaction costs have been reducing steadily, ETF trading is becoming mainstream, and automated portfolio indexing is emerging as a potential investment method. Regulators are asking for more transparency, hindering the asymmetry of information and the incentive schemes of banks. This is impacting the profitability of institutions and the economic rationale of open architectures.

Endogenous factors:

- **Strategies:** wealth management strategies need to be crafted around customer needs and can typically take two forms: cost reduction and revenue enhancement. Cost reduction is seldom achieved, while revenue enhancements are difficult to orchestrate as they often require changes in organization. Robo-technology and Goal Based Investing seem to allow banks to kill two birds with one stone, by automating the work of financial professionals (e.g., Robo-4-Advisors) to lower costs and gain operational efficiency, and tier new services with up-selling features (e.g., Gamification) by making clients' ambitions and fears the main focus, hence achieving true personalization and customer loyalty.
- **Services:** financial firms have become fairly complex over time, and so are the products that they sell. The rapid financial innovation which started in the late 1980s created operational problems and inefficiencies due to lack of back office standards, lack of defined responsibilities in the management of new services,

and lack of defined responsibilities for compliance and risk management. Regulators and the successful experience of Robo-Advisors have been reinforcing the shift towards simpler investment solutions and services (e.g., passive investment strategies). This would allow us to simplify the complexity of existing services, streamline back and front office operations, reduce costs, and enhance the dialogue between advisors and clients.

- **Systems:** banks have continuously adopted new technologies, but markets and services have been changing faster. The priorities of technology officers are integration and simplification, which can be fostered by cloud computing, cognitive analytics, and digital platforms. Technology is also making customers more mobile so that digitalization is no longer a new channel, but the new normal. The whole bank is going digital.
- **Measures of success:** banks hoping to differentiate themselves need to focus less on incremental improvements in individual metrics and more on wholesale process change, to be able to fight disruption rationally and build sustaining innovation. The "moment of truth", which is made up of the encounters with final investors, needs to be significantly improved. Behavioural analytics are the game changer, enabling banks to track social changes and stay tuned.

Clearly, Robo-Advisors' solutions pose opportunities and risks to established institutions, such as conflicts with existing channels or cannibalization of existing services. Financial institutions will therefore craft their robo-ambitions carefully and make sure that they fit current and prospective business strategy and brand.

3.6 THE DIGITAL FINANCIAL ADVISOR

Personal financial advisors are professionals who render financial services within a mandate regulated by local financial authorities and common law (e.g., FCA in the UK, FINRA in the US, ASIC in Australia), which set the tone in terms of type of services, transparency of disclaimers, and form of remuneration that they are allowed to propose. There are differences among regulations, but also common principles. This book does not provide a detailed discussion of these differences, but drafts their main attributes and discusses the international trends of advisory practices. Direct references to specific cases are provided whenever necessary. "Personal financial advisors" has been elected as generic appellation and refers to the work of those practitioners or small firms owning the rights to provide financial advice or financial planning (as the case may be) by working directly for their clients rather than representing a financial institution. Personal financial advisors can be independent or restricted (the terminology is adopted from the UK regulation, but it is used here as a general definition irrespective of the regulatory framework in which the personal financial advisor operates) . The distinction between independent and restricted refers to the form of remuneration they receive for the services they provide: independent financial advisors do not receive any rebate from any third party for the advice provided to final clients (e.g., sales loads), but depend solely on the advisory fees they ask their customers to pay. In some jurisdictions financial institutions can provide independent (e.g., fee-only) and restricted advice within the same banking perimeter (e.g., the MiFID II Regulation).

Personal financial advice is a fairly recent practice, which appeared in the late 1960s with a focus on US stock brokerage and insurance sales. Elicitation of clients' goals and monitoring of the progress of investments were not common. Following the oil crisis and the recession of the 1970s, individuals became more aware of the relevance of planning instead of solely buying and selling, and the industry started to transform. In particular, the favourable economic conditions of the 1990s facilitated the industry's expansion and prompted the first clear divide between commission based and fee-only services. Financial institutions began to see the value of using financial advisors to promote their investment products and services. The distinctive value proposition of personal financial advisors compared to traditional retail banks and online services resides in their direct and familiar relationship with taxable investors, which should enable them to anticipate, understand, and respond to their needs in a way that appears to be very personalized.

The emphasis on client relationship management restricts *de facto* the capability of traditional practitioners to manage a scaled up number of customers. Their daily workflow requires them to deal with a large amount of red tape, make decisions about money management, perform accounting tasks, research financial markets, and report investment performance. Their role seems to have gained further momentum in the aftermath of the GFC, due to a substantial loss of reputation of main street banks. Robo-Advisors have also profited from this window of opportunity and started to gather AUM at an impressive pace from 2014 to 2015. Although most of the early adopters might have come from the pool of self-directed investors, they are now pitching within the ranks of the advised clientele. However, Robo-Advisors are also transforming and have started to target institutional relationships (i.e., Robo-4-Advisors). This trend has been followed by both FinTechs and established institutions. The adoption of Robo-4-Advisors allows tech-savvy human advisors to streamline and verticalize their tasks by means of automation, and hence institutionalize the asset management aspects which are becoming somewhat commoditized (e.g., portfolio construction and portfolio rebalancing with passive investments). They can leverage automated investment services on behalf of their clients and focus their time and expertise on so-called "gamma tasks": prospecting and on-boarding new clients, following up on investment performance, engaging and amplifying on social media. Gamma tasks are particularly relevant for new entrants in the professional community of personal financial advisors, especially those targeting new generations which are more digital and social media native.

The upcoming retirement crisis will also give advisory practices a significant opportunity to strengthen and extend their businesses. Since government sponsored pension plans appear to be insufficient to fulfil the financial needs of post-retirement

Baby Boomers and younger generations, legislators are progressively transferring the burden of planning for adequate retirement income directly onto the shoulders of individuals (e.g., Australian superannuation plans) who need to be adequately advised to make decisions for long-term financial goals. Yet, the quantitative aspects related to building long-term asset allocations with income stream perspectives are not insignificant and are forcing financial advice (portfolio management) and financial planning (cash flow management) to come together in integrated solutions. The complexities of these tasks can be solved and efficiently demonstrated by extending the reach of robo-technology to treat all aspects of Goal Based Investing, as demonstrated in the second part of this book. The institutionalization of automated investment services can provide more lifeblood to high-level advisory practices as well, such as family officers and multi-family officers. They typically possess financial investment skills or reach out to financial advisory practices for all aspects of portfolio management. Yet, they still struggle to automate a large part of their investment management processes due to the multiplicity of goals and highly bespoke requirements that they have to handle. The new generation of Robo-4-Advisors also has the potential to look into these needs.

Broadly speaking, financial advice is compensated by fees or commissions:

- hourly fees for the advisory services rendered (less frequent);
- flat fees for periodic investment reviews or financial planning (e.g., advice-only practices without the responsibility of money management);
- sales loads based on invested amounts (e.g., restricted or branded practices);
- fees for assets under management (e.g., independent fee-only practices and Robo-Advisors).

To conclude, performing portfolio rebalancing of individual clients' portfolios comprising passive investments requires time and this effort might not be perceived by final clients as a differentiating element among different financial advisors. Therefore, financial advisors could use institutional robo-solutions to perform these tasks, save time, and establish branding for their clients. Institutional robo-services also provide vertical services (e.g., reporting) which would further enhance the efficiency of human advisory practices. More time can be dedicated to increasing revenues by added-value discussions with clients, goal elicitation and tracking, and complementary planning services. Robo-technology will not replace human advice altogether, but personal financial advisors and Robo-Advisors might well team up to empower independent advisory relationships and ultimately individual investors whose characteristics, needs, and transforming behaviour are discussed in the next chapter.

3.7 ASSET MANAGEMENT IS BEING DISINTERMEDIATED

Mutual funds are managed by professional investment managers, who trade securities (typically stocks, bonds, commodities, or deposits) for the most effective growth of a well identified portfolio. Each fund can be managed by an individual fund manager or a team of people, all working for the mutual fund company whose shareholders are the institutions and private individuals who have invested in the mutual fund itself.

Mutual fund companies typically include the following activities:

- **Asset research and selection:** a team of financial analysts and economists makes statistical and econometric analysis to assess the expected earnings/values of individual stocks and asset classes, to estimate the volatility and the correlation among risk factors, to envisage the economic outlook, to provide recommendations about buying or selling potentially undervalued or overvalued stocks and bonds.
- **Investment planning and implementation:** portfolio managers optimize the asset allocation according to a mandate, which restricts portfolio exposures to certain markets and strategies, or enforces the tight tracking of benchmarks.
- **Rebalancing of the fund:** realignment of the fund's exposure to the benchmark or the mandate, execution of required trades in an attempt to minimize trading costs.
- **Monitoring and risk management:** ongoing verification of the risk profile of each fund and its compliance to the mandate.
- **Marketing and reporting:** periodic reporting to market regulators, institutional and private investors, and management committees.
- **Internal audit and compliance:** ongoing auditing of operational compliance and adherence to local and international regulations.

Mutual funds are, by definition, diversified portfolios meaning they are made up of a lot of different securities whose combination complies with a mandate reflected in the strategic asset allocation. The fund allocation can deviate from the strategic view, for macro or tactical reasons, yet within the limits stated by the mandate. Fund managers trying to tame the market might leverage on their financial analysis and research experience to position portfolios more tactically, hence deviating tactical asset allocations from strategic long-term views, as represented in Figure 3.7.

The most common mutual funds policies fall into four categories, according to the nature of their strategic asset allocation: Money Market, Fixed Income, Equity, and Balanced. Money Market funds invest in liquid and short-term highly rated debt and commercial paper. Equity funds invest in common stocks and can be riskier (possibly earning more money) than other types. Fixed Income funds are made up of government and corporate securities that provide a fixed return and are usually lower risk than most equity funds. Balanced funds combine both stocks and bonds in their investment pool and offer moderate risk and return. Mutual funds can be

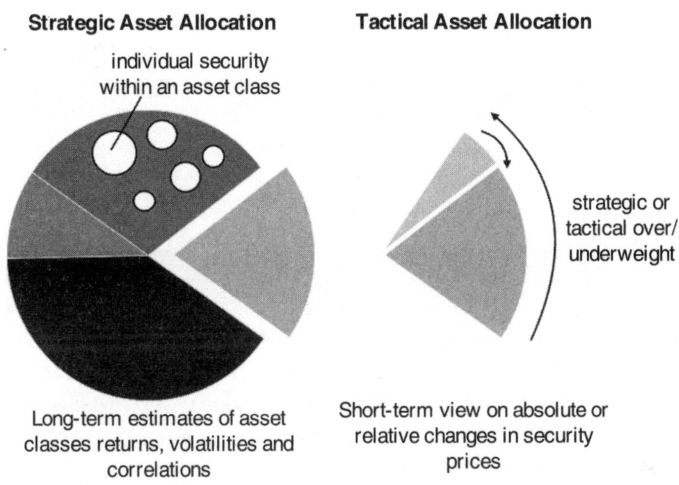

FIGURE 3.7 Strategic tactical asset allocation

open-ended (the most common case) or closed-ended. An open-ended fund is open to new investments without limit and new shares are reinvested in the portfolio (or sold back to the fund). Mutual fund shares are not sold in the traditional sense, but they are redeemed by the fund management company. With respect to closed-ended funds in contrast, only a certain number of shares can be issued for a particular fund. These shares can only be sold back to the fund when the fund itself terminates. Yet, existing shares can be sold to other investors on the secondary market. Fund managers typically distribute their fund shares through intermediaries, such as retail banks, private banks, or financial advisors.

Open architectures have been the most common distribution model, allowing wealth managers to offer their clients a broad selection of competing mutual funds. Therefore, fund managers have had to reward the intermediaries for their role in placing their shares to final investors. The costs that final investors face are called fees and can be broken down into two categories. Ongoing fees (expense ratio) are yearly costs required by fund managers to reward the work of portfolio managers (management fees), administrative costs (e.g., accounting and customer services), and marketing costs (e.g., so-called 12B-1 fee in the US). Loads are transaction fees paid when buying (front-end) or selling (back-end) shares in a fund and that mutual funds use to reward brokers and sales people; deferred fees allow them to reward investors, which do not dispose of their shares for longer periods, with lower transaction costs. No-load funds are mutual funds which distribute their shares directly without the need of third parties. Hence, they do not feature sales charges and can be seen on the internet platforms of those mutual funds selling to final investors directly.

Asset managers face three types of threats following digital solutions and robo-technology:

- **Commoditization**: the rise of Robo-Advisors has started a process of further commoditization of asset management propositions, as portfolio diversification can be conveniently built by means of inexpensive ETFs. The industry shift towards inexpensive passive management, particularly in the US, has ignited downward competition of fee levels and forced fund managers to reconsider their full cost structure.
- **Inefficient open architectures**: as regulation features the ban on retrocessions or requires much higher transparency of the embedded costs that individuals face, traditional business models are changing to favour a realignment between the propositions of asset management companies (typically product based) and private banks (typically portfolio and client based). By working much more closely, they can achieve higher cost savings and rebuild financial advice more clearly around portfolio management expertise. This convergence might affect the fate of open architectures and pose a serious threat to smaller or independent asset managers, which do not have direct access to final investors. Therefore, asset managers have started to embrace robo-technology as a way to lower operating costs (e.g., automated rebalancing of existing funds) and add B2C capabilities.
- **Client awareness**: the awareness of individual investors about the limitations of active investment management has been increasing since the GFC, particularly in the US, as well as the perception that mutual funds and ETFs are not very different in terms of potential harnessing of gross returns, while they do differ in terms of final costs. This has increased individuals' appetite for ETFs and forced institutions to rethink their revenue structures.

All these forces combine to expose asset managers to the highest risk of disruption among all of the investment management intermediaries, because robo-technology has reinforced the ETF momentum and helped to augment investors' awareness about final investment costs, as advocated by new market regulation, creating a downward spiral on operating margins. This has affected cost/income ratios and threatened their long-term profitability. The way out is twofold: asset managers need to build up better economies of scale, by merging existing practices to increase AUM per portfolio manager; they need to adopt automated portfolio rebalancing techniques (robo-technology) to replace the work of human portfolio managers, and reduce the cost structure to manage the funds. Passive asset managers have the most to lose but active asset managers will also be under significant pressure because algo-trading can embed active management rules into automated investment mechanisms. Is this all good news for ETF providers in the long term? Not really: index replication is also becoming commoditized by means of automated portfolios that can be sold directly to wealthier investors instead of ETFs.

3.8 ETF PROVIDERS AND THE PYRRHIC VICTORY

An ETF is a pooled investment vehicle with shares that can be traded throughout the day on a stock exchange at the prevailing market price, as opposed to mutual funds which can be bought and sold at their forward price (NAV) calculated at end of day. There are two types of ETFs: passively managed ETFs are index based and seek to track the performance (directly or inversely) of a specific index or a multiple of indexes; actively managed ETFs are created with a unique asset allocation to meet a particular investment object and policy. The way they are engineered and their trading features on stock exchanges, just like publicly available companies, make them cheaper investment opportunities compared to traditional mutual funds. Moreover, ETF providers can pass on most of their administrative and operating costs to brokerage firms (e.g., client services, statements, notifications, tax reports). The process of origination and distribution is referred to as the creation/redemption mechanism and sees the interaction of two actors, the sponsor and the authorized participant, as in Figure 3.8. The sponsor issues the ETF shares and lets the authorized participant buy and sell the underlying securities for a profit in order to manage the fund and receive/redeem the ETF shares in the market. This process keeps the ETF trading price in line with the fund's underlying NAV, although their price fluctuates through the trading day due to simple supply and demand. When this happens, the authorized participant can earn a risk-free arbitrage profit by buying up the underlying securities that compose the ETF and then selling ETF shares on the open market, or vice versa, and drive the price back toward fair value. Moreover, the mechanism

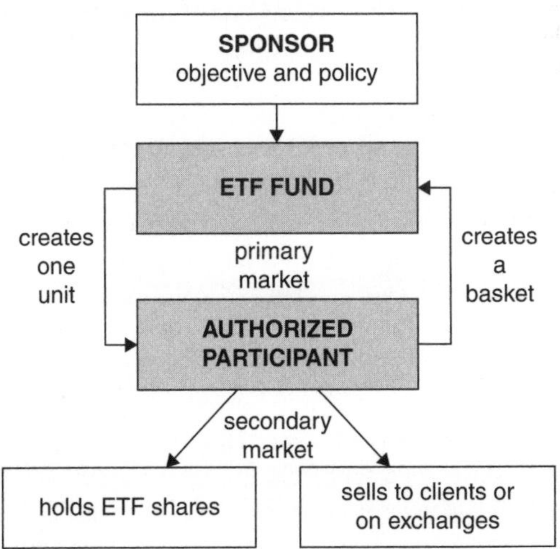

FIGURE 3.8 Creation of ETF shares

is a very cost efficient way to acquire the securities they need compared to mutual funds. When investors want to buy a mutual fund, the fund manager has to go to the market and buy securities, hence pay trading spreads and commissions which affect the expense ratio. In contrast, the authorized participant does most of the buying and selling for the ETF, paying all expenses and costs stemming from new money into or out of the fund.

The sponsor is a company or financial institution whose dedicated investment advisors choose the objective and policy of the investment vehicle, for example their benchmark and which method to use to track their returns (if index based) or which discretionary trading strategy (if actively managed). Passively managed ETFs need to track the returns of indexes, which use different methodologies of portfolio construction: weighting based on market capitalization or fundamental factors (e.g., sales or book value), factor based security selection (e.g., they screen securities according to their value, growth, or dividends), or statistical approaches (e.g., tracking error volatility). Passively managed ETFs are not necessarily a 100% replication of their benchmark, but can approximate their index by investing in a representative sample of securities in the target index to reduce operating costs or circumvent trading limitations (e.g., restrictions on ownership of certain foreign securities, or unavailability of certain fixed-income products due to low trading volumes). The authorized participant on the other hand is typically a large institutional investor, such as a market maker or broker-dealer that has entered into a legal contract with the sponsor, whose role is to facilitate the creation/redemption mechanism of ETF shares and support market demand. The authorized participant creates the basket of securities for each trading day, which are the specific quantities of securities and cash in the fund, and transfers it to the ETF so that the sponsor can issue or redeem the required number of shares, which varies based on market activity. The interaction between sponsor and authorized participant is categorized as primary market activity. The sponsor creates new shares only when the authorized participant submits an order for one or more creation units, which consist of a specified number of ETF shares. The value of the creation basket and any cash adjustment equals the value of the creation unit based on the net asset value at the end of the day on which the transaction was initiated. The authorized participant can either keep the ETF shares that make up the creation unit or sell all or part of them to its clients, or to other investors on the exchange. These sales by the authorized participant, along with any subsequent purchases and sales of these existing ETF shares among investors, are referred to as secondary market activity.

The price of an ETF share is influenced by the forces of supply and demand throughout the trading day. Therefore, imbalances in supply and demand can cause the price to deviate from its underlying value. Yet, substantial deviations tend to be short-lived due to portfolio transparency and the ability for authorized participants to create or redeem ETF shares at the NAV at the end of each trading day. Full disclosure of the portfolio enables institutional investors to observe and attempt to profit from discrepancies between the ETF's share price and its underlying value during the trading day. As indicated, they are the most convenient form of pooled trading which is currently available to individual investors and their financial advisors. Yet, their penetration among individual investors' accounts is still far from its long-term potential, due to the incentive mechanisms based on sales loads which have created an information asymmetry in favour of traditional mutual funds. This is typically defended by referring to the professional effort of intermediaries to select the best investment opportunities for their respective clients. Academic research has shown that such effort might not fully justify the costs borne by final investors (as historical performance of mutual funds is not statistically different from that of equivalent ETFs). At the same time, regulators have asked internationally for higher transparency standards on investment costs and in many cases also prescribed the full ban on retrocessions. Thus, ETF demand by private investors or their fee-only advisors soared.

However, ETF providers should be wary as well, because their advantage can soon turn into a Pyrrhic victory. Robo-technology has been exploiting diminishing trading costs of most traded securities, particularly stocks, and tax code advantages in such a way as to potentially disintermediate ETF providers as makers of convenient pooled investments. The more advantageous treatment of capital gains and losses, stemming from trading a broader set of underlying securities as opposed to a few ETFs or mutual funds, has enabled some Robo-Advisors to propose fully automated portfolios as investment solutions that track the return of indexes directly, although the debate about the long-term economic advantages of these practices is still open (besides, so far they are restricted to larger patrimonies and higher tax brackets).

3.9 VERTICALLY INTEGRATED SOLUTIONS CHALLENGE TRADITIONAL PLATFORMS

Brokers came into existence after the 1929 crash with the scope to execute stock trades on behalf of customers and quickly evolved into brokering bonds and mutual funds in return for a selling fee. In essence, brokerage firms conduct financial transactions on behalf of a client and derive their profit from commissions on orders given, although their role shifted to the oversight of sales processes and the collection and allocation of the sales commissions paid. Typically they collect a percentage of the value of each transaction, though in some cases flat fees can be charged, but some also started to provide forms of advisory services. They handle two main types of brokerage accounts: advisory and discretionary. They are only allowed to conduct transactions on advisory accounts on the explicit orders of the account holder, or under very specific instructions. On the other hand, they have much more leeway over discretionary accounts, conducting transactions not prohibited by the account holder in accordance with the holder's investment goals and the prudent man rule. In practice, most brokerage houses are in fact broker-dealer firms which provide custodian services to their clients. Clients may give orders to broker-dealers in a variety of ways: they may meet with a broker (very seldom), call on the telephone (less and less frequently), or execute orders using trading tools referred to as platforms (market practice). Trading platforms are digital tools and services that can be used to place electronic orders for financial securities with a financial intermediary (e.g., market makers, investment banks, or exchanges). Typically, they stream live market prices on which users can trade and may provide additional trading services, such as charting packages, news feeds, and account management functions. Some platforms have been specifically designed to allow individuals to gain access to financial markets that could only be accessed by financial institutions such as margin trading on derivatives (e.g., contract for difference).

The strengthening of the fiduciary standards would require them to support financial advisors with a broader set of back-office and middle-office functions, beyond traditional services offered by custodians and brokerage firms. In fact, they need to perform tasks related to portfolio account management, performance reporting, rebalancing, and client relationship management. Some Robo-Advisors have raised the competition bar, to provide vertically integrated solutions: Business to Business offers for financial advisors (i.e., Robo-4-Advisors and Robo-as-a-Service). Established platforms noticed and some responded by adding institutional robo-solutions alongside traditional custodian and brokerage services. Although robo-technology could potentially cannibalize their online trading offers, this move will give them the chance to diversify their business model at the very time change is happening, and position them to profit from the advantages of digitalization.

3.10 CONCLUSIONS

The whole supply-demand chain of the investment management industry is transforming due to new technologies (e.g., digital platforms, robo-technology, smartphones), changing investors' behaviour (e.g., social media, lower brand loyalty, peer-to-peer recommendations), tighter regulation (e.g., transparency principles, ban of inducements), and Big Data analytics. In particular, Robo-Advisors have demonstrated that disruptive innovation is at play and affects all professional supply-side actors: issuers, passive and active asset managers, ETF providers, platforms, discount brokers, private banks, retail banks, and personal financial advisors. The next chapter will review the characteristics of the demand-side, which is made up of taxable investors, and how technology can influence them or help to discern their investment behaviour.

CHAPTER 4

Social and Technology Mega Trends Shape a New Family of Taxable Investors

"Change is the process by which the future invades our lives."

—Alvin Toffler (1928–)

Three mega trends are sweeping the world and affect the wealth management industry: money is about to change hands due to a generational shift from Baby Boomers to younger heirs, at a time when wealth is polarizing horizontally and vertically (i.e., west–east and poor–rich); regulation is getting tighter, which increases fiduciary standards and affects the incentive schemes of the intermediaries; societies and individuals are progressively becoming highly interconnected (e.g., the Internet of Things), to generate an incredible amount of data that a new set of analytics can harvest to generate powerful customer insights (e.g., cognitive computing). Robo-Advisors, Goal Based Investing, and Gamification stand at the crossroads of these powerful forces, which influence the investment behaviour of individuals and affect the way financial institutions and advisors relate and function.

4.1 INTRODUCTION

Modern economies and human society at large are facing a period of unprecedented change which can be explained by the interaction of three mega trends, affecting investors' behaviour globally, with geographical differences but virtually no borders. First of all, ownership of financial assets is polarizing in the hands of the top tier of wealthy individuals, while the US and European middle class is shrinking for the first time since the Second World War. Wealth is also migrating globally towards growth markets, particularly Asia, where the middle class is instead growing. Wealth is also about to be passed to younger generations which are more techno-literate (e.g., Millennials), if not digital-native. This redistribution is creating a more diverse elite, new groups of investors, and a modification of the primary needs for the savings of families. Second, the internet has become fairly ubiquitous and this extraordinary level of connectivity, fostered by the affirmation of smartphones, has allowed us to learn new forms of social life and professional engagement (e.g., "uber-ization"). The change in consumers' behaviour is challenging traditional firms, which are embracing new technology (e.g., behavioural analytics) to reposition business strategies along the alleys of the digital village. Third, the enfolding of the global financial crisis has been economically painful for the majority of investors, reducing their appetite for risk-taking on equity markets and deteriorating their trust in financial institutions. Policy-makers have responded to the public outcry by rolling out breakthrough market regulation (e.g., FINRA rules, MiFID II, RDR, FoFA), which fosters higher transparency on intermediation costs and the packaging of risk, attempts to enhance investor protection, and realigns the basic incentives of the industry to the ultimate financial goals of individuals. Such regulatory tightening is affecting the traditional asymmetry of information of the supply-demand chain, and opens doors for a broader democratization of the investment relationship which FinTechs have quickly exploited. The combination of these forces helps to understand the rise of Robo-Advisors and the strategic relevance of Goal Based Investing, as represented in Figure 4.1.

This chapter sketches out the main traits of these revolutionary trends, and delves deeper to highlight how breakthrough technology interacts with a resulting new set of personal values.

4.2 GENERATIONAL SHIFT (X, Y, Z, AND HENRYs)

The financial industry expanded significantly after the Second World War as major economies enjoyed an unprecedented period of prosperity. Decades-long market growth accompanied the strengthening of the middle class by disposable wealth and numbers (e.g., Baby Boomers), as indicated in Figure 4.2 by the historical dynamics of the S&P 500 index.

However, today's financial environment is very different. Less than prudent financial innovation has fostered contagion effects among globalized markets and transferred an unprecedented amount of risk to individuals (e.g., the sub-prime crises). The imbalances created by market exuberance have become more pronounced, fuelled by the exponential growth of capital inflows and the speed of electronic trading. Price corrections are more frequent and severe, questioning the validity of common assumptions like the long-term relationship between the performance of stocks and fixed income markets. As individuals and companies have learned to depend more on financial markets, particularly in the US, market crises have widespread impact on the real economy and sometimes social security. All of this happens at the very

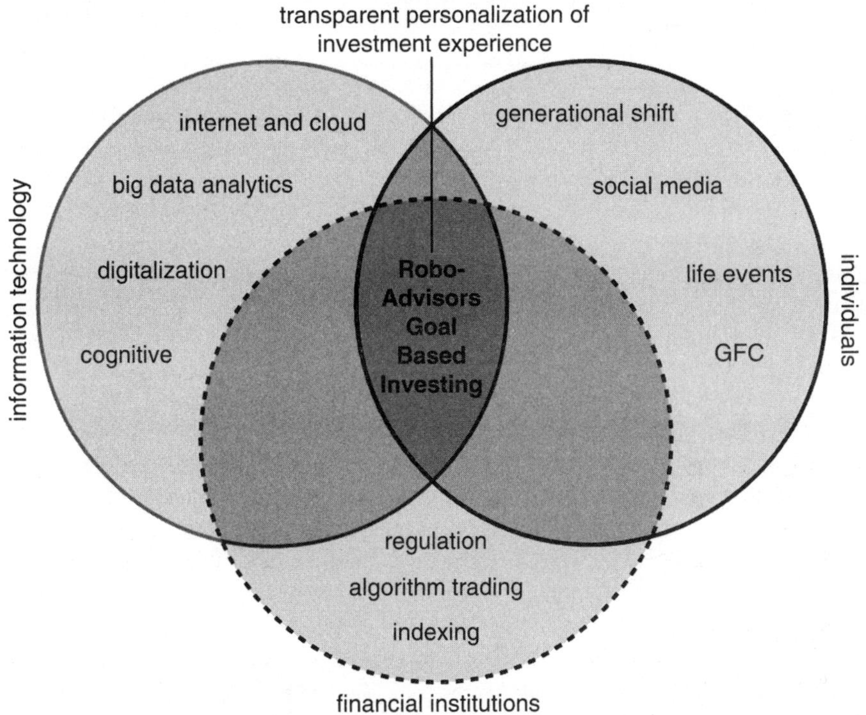

FIGURE 4.1 Innovation and mega trends

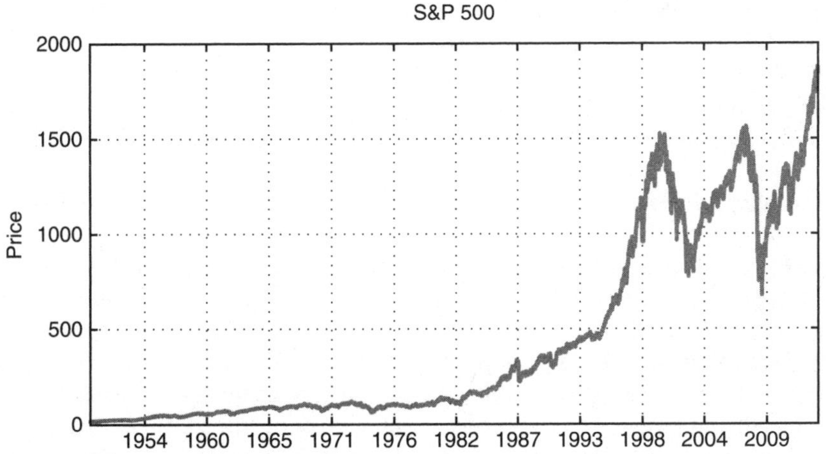

FIGURE 4.2 S&P 500 time series

same time that the Baby Boomers have started to retire, draw down from their wealth at various points of the market cycle, or pass it to the next generations of more tech-savvy taxable investors. A very large portion of the affluent and mass affluent population will depend upon reduced or uncertain retirement income, because the progressive deterioration of the economic cycle and the contraction of the active workforce have started to put government sponsored pension plans under unsustainable stress. Policy-makers have addressed this problem by requiring individuals to be more responsible during their active working life and invest in private plans which are usually financed by compulsory employers' contributions and tax-deferral advantages. Yet, the unintended consequence of the shift from defined benefits to defined contributions has been to add long-term financial risk to the potential performance of retirement savings, which further exacerbates the dependance of basic social security on the fate and cycle of the financial markets. A demographic divide is also building since the world population has been growing steadily but not evenly: developing countries are adding to most of the increase, while mature economies are experiencing very low birth rates. This is creating a dichotomy between the needs of an ageing population in the US, Canada, Europe, Australia, and Japan, compared to the "youth dividend" of growth markets, particularly in Asia. Therefore, incumbent institutions are challenged to expand fast and reposition their brands and operations in diverging environments which are more challenging than ever before, and have to contend with: a severe loss of reputation caused by the global financial crisis; a shrinking middle class, which has a lower portion of available income to invest in financial products, or can no longer afford the fees of traditional services; an ageing population, which needs to de-cumulate from pre-retirement investments; a change of ownership of financial resources from traditional Baby Boomers to younger and more tech-savvy cohorts (X and Y); and a diverging world stage. The United Nations Joint Staff Pension Fund report (2013) provides an insightful description of the behavioural differences among generations:

- **Traditionalists (1925 to 1945):** the Veterans' generation is made up of individuals who experienced economic and political uncertainty culminating in the Second World War, which taught them to become hard working, financially conservative, and cautious. Typically, they like rules, do not like change, and are fairly risk-averse.
- **Baby Boomers (1945 to 1965):** this generation grew up in a healthy post-war economy. They generally value hard work and own the bulk of middle-class wealth in mature economies.
- **Generation X (1965 to 1980):** this generation witnessed the birth of the information age and grew up with a high rate of mixed-culture, mixed-race, and blended families. While Boomers literally "lived to work", Generation X "has been working to live", as they were reared in the shadow of more prominent older generations. Since work life is more a means to an end, they are quite goal-orientated and dedicated, yet value the freedom to do it their way which

is reflected in being more self-directed when it comes to financial investments. They also express higher techno-literacy.

- **Generation Y or Millennials (1980 to 2000):** this generation has been supported for longer by their parents, due to rising costs of housing and education. They have been encouraged to be opinionated, yet with a higher degree of relativism, which makes them more open to challenging the status quo, established brands, and incumbent institutions. More than Generation X, they have grown up with computers and the internet as an important part of their lives. Due to their experience in a global and networked society, they are highly connected through social networks, instant messaging systems, and blogs. They tend to like diversity more, might lack the skills for dealing with difficult situations, and hence favour immediacy and simplicity.
- **Generation Z or digital-native (after 2000):** Google already existed when they opened their eyes for the first time. Too young to be a target of financial services, they pose a series of long-term concerns to traditional wealth managers because, being more than techno-literate, they are truly digital beings. They are therefore even more open to accepting a full disintermediation of financial services by newcomers powered by robo-technology.

Generations X and Y also tend to experience many more life events compared to conservative Baby Boomers: they have their first children later in life, they change jobs and relocate more frequently, they might not own a house, they might have to take care of their children for longer, and at the same time assist elderly parents. This seems to lead to more varied investment requirements, or a broader set of investment goals to be fulfilled at once. Moreover, Millennial HENRYs (High Earning, Not Rich Yet) account for a significant portion of wealth owned by new generations and seem to feature even lower dependency on human engagement when it comes to financial advice, with a higher propensity to adopt leaner, digital, and "any time, anywhere" investment solutions such as Robo-Advisors can offer. Since new generations are more aspirational in their approach to life and consumption, traditional firms are asked to revise their long-term approaches to investment and relationship management, and adopt more transparent and engaging customer experiences to position their services along the lines of the generational shift. The disruptive self-directed approach of Robo-Advisors, the personalization of Goal Based Investing, and the emotional engagement of Gamification seem to provide valuable answers to the needs and values of these generations, and allow the creation of a captive digital experience.

4.3 ABOUT TRANSPARENCY, SIMPLICITY, AND TRUST

The changes ushered in by the generational shift are not confined to a different propensity and ability to use digital tools and communicate virtually, but extend to the values that individuals possess and which modify their expectations when dealing with personal investments and financial advisors. Social networks have made peering more flexible, so that people are more likely to associate with professional or social networks and trust "people like me". As news streams in at unprecedented speed, opinions and values can be forged and exchanged fast (e.g., viral messages). Therefore, there is a modification of how trust in organizations is built within communities, businesses, and brands. Trust can be established with digital marketing, but can be easily destroyed by word of mouth and negative sentiment on social media. Financial institutions, which suffered a severe loss of reputation during the GFC, are struggling to rebuild a trustworthy image and seem to be fairly slow to embrace social media to their advantage, compared to other industries. FinTechs instead have demonstrated that banking brands can be challenged with lean budgets, digital solutions, and smart marketing. Personal financial advisors themselves have the opportunity to use social media to establish professional trust by creating blogs and sharing actionable content, thus enlarging their network and engaging their clients more effectively. The web is a key marketplace for peering, prospecting, and content sharing. Regulators are imposing higher transparency on investment costs and individuals are learning to compare services in terms of their full costs and added value. The internet is clearly facilitating these comparisons and favours businesses whose offers come across as simpler and more intuitive. In such an environment, user-friendly digital access and upfront asset allocations seem to be winning propositions. The complexity of investment decision-making can be simplified and represented graphically to enhance intuitive understanding of otherwise complex mathematical relationships. Also tabular representation of risks and opportunities seems to be more effective than verbose legalese. Yet, financial institutions clearly struggle to find the right balance between compliance and red-tape, digital ergonomics, mitigation of legal risks, and intuitiveness of investment propositions.

The "time-squarization" of financial news has become a clear problem. The overabundance of financial data is not optimal, and can confuse investors and affect their decision-making. As news bounces on radio channels, televisions, social media, billboards, and magazines, individuals cannot easily filter out what is relevant from what is noise. Smart spin doctors can convey messages and prop up perceptions that exploit or generate sentiment, and hence influence public opinion. Financial services are not exempt and often find themselves in the middle of the storm as markets and economies go through the cycle. Every uptick of the market, no matter how exuberant, is welcomed as inevitable while every downtick is described as the destruction of public value. Wealth managers are therefore required to filter information conveyed to their respective customers, and make sure that their message is properly received and that clients can focus only on those elements which are relevant and actionable. Most Robo-Advisors attempt to engage customers in long-term investing, tempering the emotional impact of market news and directing investors' attention to their long-term message instead.

Advisory firms need to focus on two key principles to mitigate the "time-squarization" of financial news: information needs to be personal (hence relevant) and actionable.

- **Personalization:** hints conveyed to investors must be relevant given existing portfolios, what they search for on the web, declared or most likely goals, personal characteristics, and behaviour of their peers. This would allow wealth managers to approach clients with relevant content at the right time of their life, enhancing the probability that such communication is impactful and adds value to the relationship.
- **Actionability:** any piece of information conveyed to investors should lead to the potential generation of a trade, or a request for more financial advice, particularly if human advisors cannot act as a filter or translator for financial news, which is the case with self-directed investors.

Therefore, personalizing the informative context can significantly enhance experience to generate more business. This can be achieved by deploying behavioural analytics:

- log-in sensors: firms can learn customers' habits such as preferred log-in time and frequency, to reach out with the most appropriate schedule.
- "googling" sensors: institutions can track what investors search for (e.g., products, news, documents) when they engage with applications, and customize the display to show similar elements in subsequent web sessions.
- investment relevance: applications can highlight financial news which is related to the risks and opportunities affecting the bets in clients' portfolios.
- peer relevance: investors can be made aware of what their peers buy, sell, or search for in order to reinforce a desired behaviour or any commercial message.
- social media: analytics can follow clients on social media and garner insights into their mood, topics of interest, and relationships by means of deep learning and analytics for personality insights. This would help to create the right personalized content to reach out and engage at the right time.

It's about content, of course! Yet, the most important element of content customization would be the personalization of the heart and soul of the investment experience itself; that is why and what we should buy or sell. That is portfolio modelling based on Goal Based Investing principles.

4.4 THE COGNITIVE ERA

The ambition of creating a knowledge power house is not new to human history and finds a germane example in the Library of Alexandria, built in the Hellenistic period which followed the life of Alexander the Great (356–323 BC), whose inspiration and visionary belief in a multi-cultural society transformed his world into a cosmopolitan stage. The Library was the apex of a knowledge based intelligentsia, which attempted to consolidate into a single space an impressive quantity of data, knowledge, and scientific insights. Today it would not be possible to store within a single centre the amount of data that humans and their machines generate, nor would it be possible to distinguish with clarity what is relevant for individuals or decision-makers. Big Data analytics seem to be the solution to the challenging tasks of deriving insights from such an impressive informative space. From being silent servants of human-designed processes, computers are turning into business partners, virtually capable of understanding human narrative, interpreting images, and learning to draw non-obvious correlations across an immense amount of unformatted data. Cognitive computing can embrace all aspects of the Internet of Things, as Big Data analytics create the logical relation among any pieces of information that our digital world exchanges and generates. Banks themselves are creating new job functions, such as data scientists, to tackle Big Data and optimize their commercial propositions to final investors. Nowadays, cognitive expertise can go hand in hand with human advice.

"What is Big Data?"

Big Data is a broad term to indicate information sets which are so large or complex that they make traditional processing tools inadequate. We primarily refer to the business challenges to exploiting data abundance and achieving more accurate predictions of market trends and investor behaviour: collecting, searching, analysing, reducing, visualizing, and complying with privacy rules. Industry analysts usually define Big Data by referring to the 3Vs work of Douglas Laney (2001): Volume, Velocity, and Variety.

- **Volume:** fast growing data volumes cover the storage of transaction based data, social media streaming of unstructured data, sensor based and machine-to-machine inputs and outputs. As storage costs have been decreasing over recent years, today's main problem posed by excessive data volume refers to the determination of relevance within large datasets and how to use analytics to create value.
- **Velocity:** most organizations face time challenges, as data streams in at unprecedented speed and must be dealt with in a timely manner.
- **Variety:** data can be generated as structured representations in traditional databases such as financial transactions, or unstructured formats such as pdf documents, tweets, emails, videos, and audios. Governing such a variety is something many organizations still grapple with.

The Big Data revolution is changing the way wealth management institutions shape their strategic approach to decision-making and business intelligence, as shown in Figure 4.3.

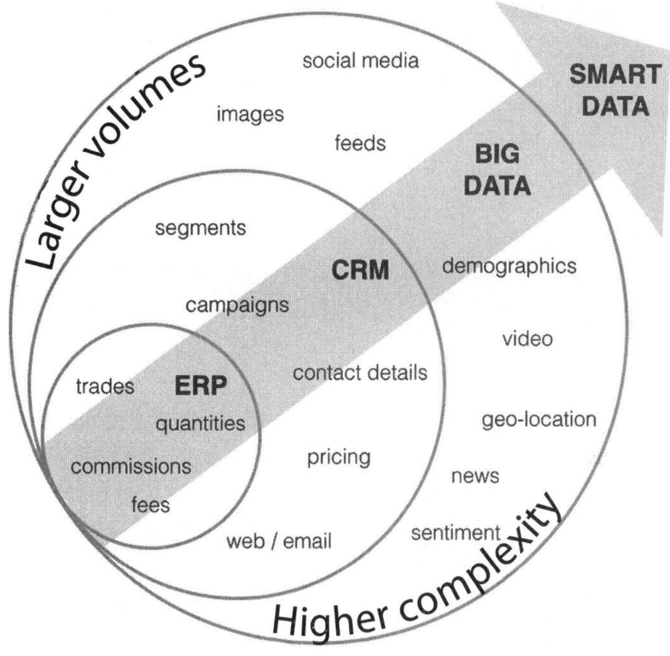

FIGURE 4.3 From Big Data to Smart Data

Enterprise Resource Planning tools (ERP) have been used traditionally to optimize cost/income ratios by focusing on detailed transaction data to increase sales volumes or profitability. Since the supply-demand chain of the wealth management industry is not a straightforward mechanism, greater importance had been assigned to the use of Client Relationship Management tools (CRM), which provide a standardized approach to storing and sharing information about investors' data and their interactions with advisors. Thorough analysis of such data has traditionally been performed to increase the effectiveness of advisory campaigns and human relationships, to improve customer retention and make customer relations more efficient. Big Data has introduced a new approach to business intelligence, which broadens the spectrum of customer analytics to all possible information about individuals and families as they are part of communities, social media platforms, demographic cohorts, or peer groups. Therefore, the investigation of such an enlarged dataset can strengthen the positioning of the wealth management offer and enables one to act on sentiment. Clearly, such an analytical challenge cannot be handled by traditional business management systems based on relational databases, desktop statistics, or visualization packages. Businesses require new forms of data analytics to uncover large hidden values from datasets that are diverse and on a massive scale. Machine learning appears to be the most revolutionary approach, since it does not require filtering data, but attempts to detect patterns or correlations among pieces of information, to identify the most adequate answer to a well-defined knowledge based problem. Digital technology makes visualization problems more approachable, allowing us to contextualize cognitive answers and drill down into Big Data datasets with graphical representations so that a new terminology seems to be arising within the business community: Smart Data.

Since Robo-Advisors were born at the intersection between finance and technology, they are digital solutions by birth and speak the language of social media. Their positioning in front of the broader public is fairly agile compared to traditional wealth managers. Most importantly, they have learned to garner information about target customers by tiering them not solely on disposable wealth, but primarily by analysing their investment behaviour, their level of techno-literacy and their social media interaction. Therefore, they are well poised to benefit the most from Smart Data and behavioural analytics, and they can rank first adopters of machine learning to strengthen clients' on-boarding mechanisms: by plugging in cognitive dialogues and replacing the current "tick-the-box" type of profiling questionnaires. They can be first adopters of blockchain technology to retrieve information about an individual's demographics and turn account opening and aggregation into a much faster and less painful experience for taxable investors.

4.5 CONCLUSIONS

Robo-technology and Goal Based Investing have been gaining momentum due to a concomitance of factors (i.e., mega trends) ranging from innovation in technology, demographical shifts, higher fiduciary standards, to the progressive digitalization of everyday life. We have presented what Robo-Advisors are, we have discussed the threats faced by the industry, and we have provided insights into some mega trends. Having discerned the forces at play under the crustal plate of the wealth management fault, the next chapter attempts to draft its future landscape above ground while the tremors of the digital earthquake are still occurring.

CHAPTER 5

The Industry's Dilemma and the Future of Digital Advice

"There is nothing permanent except change"

—Heraclitus (535–475 BC)

This chapter concludes the first part and discusses the future outlook of the industry, the puzzle of the digital revolution, the actions required to solve it, the transformation of Robo-Advisors into Digital-Advisors: Robo-4-Advisors and Robo-as-a-Service. Final investors take a progressively more central role in a personalized investment experience, incentive mechanisms adjust to favour fee-only and mitigate compliance costs. Digital engagement and cognitive analytics allow the new client visual to go live with Goal Based Investing principles and reinvigorate the original spirit of the industry: clients come first!

5.1 INTRODUCTION

Unquestionably, the mission of the industry should be the provision of investment services to individuals and families, with the goal of optimizing and fulfilling their financial well-being over time. However, business reality is not always aligned with this foundation. Private investors have found it notoriously difficult to make investment decisions, financial intermediaries have ultimately enjoyed an advantageous asymmetry of information with regard to direct and indirect conflicts of interests and the costs embedded in their services. Their placing power has exacerbated the product-driven aspects of traditional advice, steering the main focus away from clients' actual goals and risk tolerance. The economic incentives granted to involved professionals (e.g., bonuses, sales loads) favoured volumes and transactions over investor satisfaction. The damage to reputation suffered by traditional firms during the GFC reinforced the call for tighter market regulation (e.g., FINRA rules, MiFID II, RDR, FoFA), which has significantly increased the cost of compliance and severely reduced their potential profitability by enforcing higher transparency on costs and conflicts of interest. Nowadays, the unveiling of the asymmetry of information is forcing wealth managers to rethink their product-driven approach at a time of declining margins, and establish a healthier relationship with final customers based on clearer client/portfolio-centric methods. This transformation is anything but easy! Incumbent organizations rely on established hierarchical structures which are modelled around decades-long commercial motivations. They are not aligned with the strategic imperatives brought forward by disruptive technology and demographical changes. But the epicentre of the earthquake sits in the war rooms of regulatory bodies and policy-makers, and their battle to embrace technology shifts, protect investors, and remain pro-business. Paradoxically, regulation is meant to act as a counter-balance to incumbents' economic interests compared to those of taxable investors, but can also be a barrier to entry for smaller and innovative contenders. Robo-technology and customers' analytics have helped FinTech innovators to break through even in such a highly regulated industry. The discussion in this book about Goal Based Investing questions the remaining though relevant aspects of traditional finance and provides a way out of the impasse in the "race to zero". Smart compliance can become a competitive advantage to capture market share and generate higher revenues.

This chapter discusses key business dilemmas and presents the future outlook of an industry which is transforming rapidly towards fee-only models and more digital financial advisors, capable of embedding automated investment services into their practices as Robo-Advisors become institutionalized. They also feel the pressure to transform and counter the resurgent competition of incumbents, and thus launch Robo-4-Advisors and Robo-as-a-Service platforms.

5.2 WEALTH MANAGEMENT FIRMS: GO DIGITAL OR DIE

There is no generally accepted definition of wealth management firms, but two main criteria are traditionally used: the constitution of their client base (e.g., assets under management or advice) and their modality of interaction with clients (depth of personal relationships and broader scope of services). This does not seem to hold any longer. First of all, financial institutions typically divide their clientele according to the 1 million dollar rule, as in the wealth pyramid of Figure 3.5: below this figure would be retail banking, of which affluent clients owning more than a hundred thousand dollars, above private banking. Wealth management typically refers to the services provided to clients above a hundred thousand dollars: affluent, HNW and UHNW. This triage has been progressively criticized because banks have realized that affluent customers had been somewhat underserved and they have started looking for ways to institutionalize the private banking relationship with a top down approach:

making the personalization of private banking affordable to less wealthy individuals. Robo-Advisors moved faster with a bottom up approach, by launching industrialized solutions that appeal to customers of retail banking, but observed that the same services were attracting affluent and wealthier investors. Second, with respect to their modality of interaction, Maude (2010) identifies three attributes: the breadth and depth of the relationship that wealth managers have with their clients; the products and services provided (e.g., tax advisory expertise, alternative investments); and the specific objectives of wealthy clients (e.g., investment performance, wealth transfer). But this criterion does not seem entirely appropriate any longer either. Younger generations are starting to manage personal and professional relationships differently from traditional customers. They demand "any time, anywhere" access, they face a broader variety of life events and therefore possess a variety of interdependent financial goals to be fulfilled at once. Therefore, the relevance of investing with a clearer goal perspective is soaring across all client segments. As a result, the line dividing retail and private banking is getting blurred, as well as the divide between retail bank customers and affluents. Firms are testing new analytics to perform client segmentation according to individuals' techno-literacy, social behaviour, personality, and goals more than their wealth or the dedication of appropriate advisory workforce. This fits the transition away from a cost-orientated model (e.g., sales loads) towards an income-orientated approach (e.g., fee-only advice). But it causes due concerns within incumbent organizations because the adoption of a client/portfolio-centric model does not seem to be aligned with traditional incentive mechanisms. Moreover, existing sales staff might be under-skilled to operate in a portfolio/client advice modality. Once again, cognitive technology might help to raise both the depth and efficiency of a new breed of Digital-Advisors. A more refined client segmentation is essential to counterbalance the reduced placing power of distribution networks, so that digital branding of products and services becomes strategic. The catalogues of open architectures look too crowded to steer interest towards higher margin yet simplified services. There will be less space for marketing or advisory campaigns based on the next hot product or market driver (e.g., Asian stocks), to favour more holistic and hopefully gamified goal based propositions.

The need to combine traditional triage with added-value services in ways that are convenient and engaging will lead to the generation of a mixed environment where Robo-Advisors and personal financial advisors coexist, and also interact by means of digital advice, which is a hybrid of human advice and Robo-4-Advisors (as in Figure 5.1).

Are transforming retail and private banks at risk of getting stuck in the middle of the crossing? Transforming at once into a fully fledged fee-only business seems unfeasible given organizational resistance and a gap in technology and education. Yet, retreating to the product-driven stronghold would expose cost/income sustainability to unbearable risks, as clients move out and compliance costs sky-rocket. The bank of the future is not asked but forced to be truly digital, to offer a predominance of fee-only services, to gain operational efficiency by broader robo-automation, and to

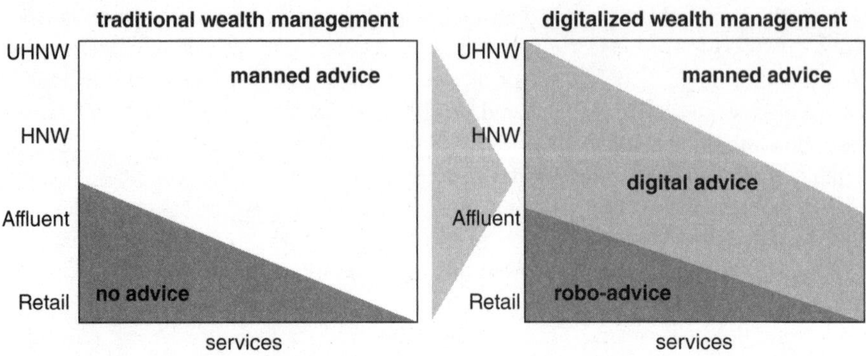

FIGURE 5.1 Digitalized wealth management

embrace goal based holistic approaches by which to build a balanced, compliant, personalized, and added-value dialogue with final investors. But spending to go digital will not be enough without a change in the philosophy driving the making of personal investments: technology and finance must innovate together. Goal Based Investing is the only path ahead to give substance to the digital revolution and increase business margins in a competitive digital industry. Four strategic imperatives can be discerned: go digital, become income-orientated, go robo-technology, embrace Goal Based Investing.

First, digitalize! The adoption of digital technology will allow banks to democratize the access to their services and enhance customer experience. Although design thinking is a must, wealth management digitalization is not purely about aesthetics and ergonomics, but primarily about effective personalization of the whole investment experience, which is a blend of robo-technology and Goal Based Investing.

Second, become income orientated! Investments in innovative technology and proactive compliance can become effective only if business incentives are realigned to client/product-centric propositions. Banks will profit the most from the digitalization challenge only if they prove to possess a flexible corporate culture, capable of embracing the transformation of organizations and processes.

Third, go robo-technology! Robo-advice is not just a buzzword for research analysts and social media commentators, but an operational imperative for those banks capable of going digital, prioritizing wealth management offers, simplifying back-office operations, and automating key parts of their workflow. Yet, launching Robo-Advisors targeting customers of retail banking or Millennials is not a good enough strategy because banks are not single minded businesses, clients have more than one need and, most importantly, human advice and robo-advice are not incompatible but can sit together. Learning from the elements of automation that Robo-Advisors have put forward is their real opportunity since robo-technology would be more relevant to them than outright robo-advice (as in Figure 5.2). It is not about Robo-Advisors, but robo-technology.

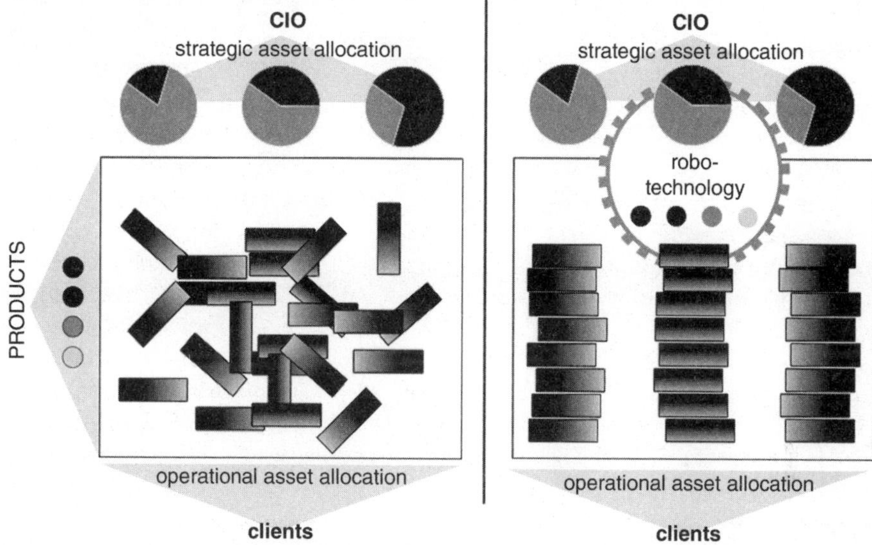

FIGURE 5.2 Robo-technology at the centre of asset allocation

Fourth, embracing Goal Based Investing is key for innovative investment experiences to address holistic well-being and direct transparent dialogues about personal ambitions, fears, and opportunities. This shift requires banks to update investment policies of portfolio construction and abandon the asset management perspective (e.g., benchmarking) to embrace Goal Based Investing, Rebalancing, and Reporting as presented in the second part of this book.

5.3 ASSET MANAGEMENT FIRMS: LESS PASSIVE, MORE ACTIVE

The fate and transformation of retail and private banks affects the operating model of the asset management industry as well. Asset managers are possibly confronting the biggest disruptive threat among the players of the supply-demand chain, but the smart ones might also be front runners in the race to zero if they can embrace robo-technology. Asset managers are still the basic manufacturers of most investment products and can transform into very competitive Robo-Advisors. Why bother? First of all, because the regulatory shift, which seeks to shed light on their opaque payment model, is squeezing their profitability and places them at odds with the changing incentive schemes of traditional firms and distribution networks. Second, because asset allocation has been progressively commoditizing and there has been growing criticism about the fairness of the price/benefit relationship of mutual funds compared to cheaper forms of passive investing (e.g., ETFs). Third, because traditional platforms might not provide them with a good enough distribution channel: the shift from product sales to portfolio propositions triggers a simplification of their overcrowded shelf, and forces them to focus on a smaller number of funds which compete more fiercely on branding and costs. Fourth and last, because even those asset managers capable of differentiating their investment ideas (e.g., active fund managers) might not remain successful due to rule based algorithms which can disrupt their operating model. As a consequence, while large manufacturers and distributors of mutual funds can harness further economies of scale by launching conveniently branded Robo-Advisors, robo-technology is seriously threatening mid-sized and undifferentiated asset managers. They are asked to do two things: scale their business and reach out directly to investors.

"Merge and acquire" is relevant to remaining sustainable in a price competitive world.

Geting closer to final investors is an imperative, which can be achieved by launching Robo-Advisors or signing strategic alliances with existing digital solutions.

Traditional asset managers seem to encounter a cultural obstacle because a culture gap still exists between them and wealth managers. Building portfolios to tame the markets (e.g., alpha seeking) is not necessarily aligned with the needs of private bankers to manage wealth through the cycle. The necessary adoption of Goal Based Investing principles would further diverge the perspectives of these professional players. Asset managers might find it difficult to transform from providers of products into providers of automated portfolio solutions based on their own funds, although this would be their best chance to become more integrated with digital distribution channels and provide price competitive services which FinTechs and direct banking might not be able to compete with.

5.4 ROBO-PLATFORMS: LESS TRANSACTIONS, MORE PORTFOLIOS

The existence of trading platforms dates back to 1973 when The Society for Worldwide Interbank Financial Telecommunications (SWIFT) was established to facilitate a standard approach to messaging and payment data processing among international banks. Advances in technology have facilitated the affirmation of electronic exchanges against trading pitches, the NYSE trading floor being the last relevant human pitch remaining. The 1990s saw the establishment and rise of many electronic platforms to facilitate self-directed trading by non-professional individuals. With the bursting of the Dot-Com bubble and higher volatility brought about by September 11th, e-trading platforms were pushed to specialize and service the most experienced clientele: nowadays most platforms provide desktop applications which resemble professional trading systems. Recently, the open architecture model has become an essential approach to grant access to investment opportunities, particularly in the

US where platforms support a wide range of distribution channels (brokers, personal financial advisors, insurers, asset managers). Europe has so far had a patchy marketplace: the UK's distribution network is geared by platforms, the Nordic countries have a predominance of closed architectures, while continental Europe is fairly mixed. The progressive reduction in the predominance of universal banks within the European distribution market should facilitate the growth of personal financial advisors, and thus the propositions of platforms. Asian platforms are also emerging as competitive distribution channels. However, in a more digital and fee-only world financial advisors are progressively less "incentivized sellers" and more "sophisticated buyers" starting to demand more robo-advice for advisors (i.e., Robo-4-Advisors), based on long-term portfolio management with passive investments instead of idiosyncratic trades, which puts pressure on platforms' pay-per-tick margins. Digital education of self-directed investors is also growing more relevant. Investors are becoming more informed about price differences, can access directly a broad range of financial information, and feel a lot more comfortable managing their portfolios online compared to the 1990s. Machine learning and Gamification could strengthen platforms to improve and become more profitable, especially in fast growing markets like Asia.

Therefore, platforms have a clear competitive advantage as they are already embedded in the work of many financial advisors and could master the digital revolution by engaging in a robo-transformation of their business model, hence turning into vertically integrated Robo-Platforms.

5.5 DIGITAL-ADVISORS: EMPOWERED CUSTOMIZATION

Financial advisors are a very influential factor in the makeup of investors' portfolios, as they sit at the forefront of the wealth management relationship and are asked to advise clients through the cycle on a broad range of goals related to their financial well-being. According to a recent study on Canadian households' portfolios by Foerster, Linnainmaa, Melzer and Previtero (2014) advised clients take statistically more risk in their asset allocations, thereby raising expected returns, although there seems to be limited evidence of customization. Advisors seem to direct clients into similar portfolios independent of their clients' risk preferences and stage in the life cycle. Social trends are demonstrating that personalization is becoming progressively relevant to younger generations, and thus must be embedded within the full advisory experience for advisors to stay competitive. Therefore, the main challenge they face is to find the right balance between a progressive commoditization or robotization of portfolio management and a high perception of personalized advice. All for the right fees! Individuals are truly becoming more comfortable managing their wealth online but they also need to be guided through a process of self-directed customization. The synthesis of these conflicting desires can be termed **empowered customization**, which means being guided through the investment decision-making process instead of being taught about it. Both Robo-Advisors and personal financial advisors are competing in this space. If you cannot beat them, join them. Hence the rise of Robo-4-Advisors which aim to create a new professional being, the Digital-Advisor or cyborg, as many commentators like to call it. The advantages of merging personal advice and robo-technology are not limited to portfolio management and profiling, but extend to prospecting. Individuals increasingly rely on social media and peer-to-peer recommendations to learn investment ideas and trust relationships, instead of their being passed on from father to son. Therefore, old-school advisors will suffer the most, as they find it difficult to reach out in a digital world, while younger and techno-literate professionals could exploit new technology to their advantage by penetrating communities of potential clients by means of social media networking. Digital-Advisors could therefore benefit from the vertical integration offered by Robo-4-Advisors or new Robo-Platforms, thus outsourcing the building blocks of portfolio rebalancing to robo-solutions and freeing up valuable time for "gamma tasks": social media relationships, blogging, on-boarding of new customers, walking clients through their life cycle, proactively engaging with their evolving ambitions, risk tolerances, and multiple financial goals. Three drivers of transformation affect the practices of personal financial advisors and three recommendations can be given to master digital change: focus on the generational divide, have a digital life, take care of retirement.

First, master the generational shift! Wealth is about to change hands as Baby Boomers retire, de-cumulate from their investments, or pass them to younger generations. This creates a divide between the approach and fate of financial advisors because new generations are more likely to change their provider of financial advice than older cohorts. According to a study by Cerulli Associates (2013) 43% of US advisors are over 55. As Baby-Boomer advisors are servicing a more mature population, they might not feel compelled to embrace change as they themselves are approaching retirement. New entrants can grab this chance and target both inheritance money as well as the new generation of HENRYs.

Second, have a digital life! Robo-technology allows verticalization of the wealth management workflow of small firms, facilitates faster on-boarding of prospects, offers recognized digital branding, and adds efficient digital dialogues with final investors. Although first adopters of robo-advice seem to come from the pool of already self-directed investors, more than personally advised AUM, FinTechs are posed to attract a much larger portion of advised AUM by competing with those professionals who are not embracing modern CRM competences. Therefore, embedding Robo-4-Advisors within human advice saves time from red-tape and routine, and allows more focus on "gamma tasks" to retain customers, on-board prospects, improve reporting, justify advisory fees, and optimize cost/income. Advisors can learn to run blogs to become relevant and share content with their clients and prospects in ways which are more relational and less prescriptive. Clients might appreciate learning what others do more than being told what to do. Digital presence gives advisors the means to stay relevant, but also prove their propositions by crafting social media nudges.

Third, take care of retirement! The wealthy population has been ageing fast, life after retirement has been extending favourably, while government finances have been exposed to unprecedented stress. Taxable investors are becoming more aware that government sponsored schemes might not be enough to sustain their purchasing power during their golden years, while retirement plans linked to the dynamics of financial markets have created excessive exposure of investors' nest eggs to the financial cycle. This is creating a broader request for personal advice on long-term investing, which is typical of financial planning solutions, but requires higher competences of financial markets, which is typical of financial advice. Digital technology and Gamification offer solutions to visualize the impact of investment decision-making in the long term, which human advisors should embrace to enrich clients' decision-making. Due to the behavioural and psychological complexities of managing holistic discussions with individuals and families about long-term financial planning, Digital-Advisors seem to have a competitive advantage compared to self-directed offers, as long as their pricing point is attractive. Financial advice and financial planning can converge to forge a very competitive workforce of independent Digital-Advisors.

5.6 ROBO-ADVISORS: BE HUMAN, BE VIRTUAL, TAKE CARE OF RETIREMENT

FinTechs have started a revolution in the banking industry on a global scale, since they leverage technology to anticipate the transformation of the business models that banks themselves will have to chase and comply with higher fiduciary standards and clients' digital behaviour. Robo-Advisors have found a fertile terrain in the US, given its higher penetration of personal financial advisors, broader reliance on retail distribution platforms, higher financial literacy of taxable investors, much more open debate about banking practices and asset management weaknesses, and a more vibrant usage of social media for online peering across all generations. Although their portion of total AUM is still lagging the trillion target to pay back the bills, venture capitalists have been pouring in substantial money by recognizing their highly disruptive potential. Recent evidence shows that incumbents adopting robo-technology can on-board AUM at an even faster pace, as shown in Figure 5.3.

The fact is that, while FinTech Robo-Advisors initially exploited social media to attract customers, and still use it to strengthen their brands and provide education on long-term investing, marketing campaigns on traditional media cannot be avoided altogether and they are quite expensive.

Therefore, much capital will have to be dedicated to marketing instead of pushing ahead on competing innovation to stay relevant against incumbent firms. Most importantly, as incumbent institutions embrace robo-technology the distinctive message of disruptive FinTechs tends to be diluted. Regulators are also looking more closely into the phenomenon, which will soon translate into higher compliance costs. Therefore,

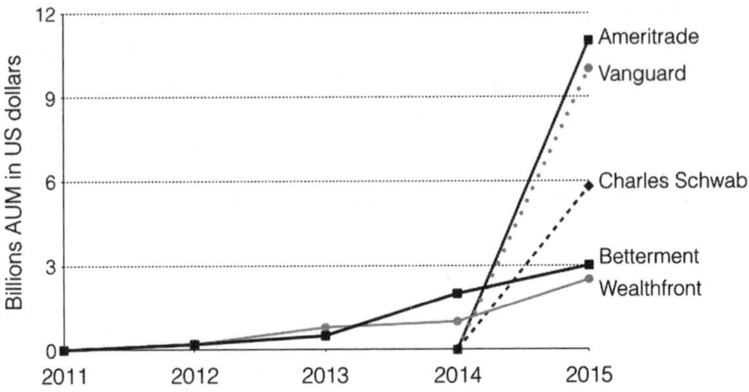

FIGURE 5.3 Growth of US Robo-Advisors

the most compelling challenges of FinTech Robo-Advisors can be summarized as follows:

- fund higher marketing costs for every new client acquired;
- abandon the race to zero;
- differentiate better against robo-peers;
- provide multiple services, without losing on simplicity and effectiveness;
- face higher compliance costs.

What to do? Three trends can be identified as opportunities to match the competition, stay ahead, and grow: go human (Robo-4-Advisors), go virtual (Robo-as-a-Service), chase retirement money (Robo-Retirement).

First, Robo-4-Advisors will help digital players to "go digital" and institutionalize their offer by leveraging AUM penetration of personal financial advisors.

Second, Robo-as-a-Service will help digital players to "go virtual", that is offer their digital and automation capabilities as services to mid-small financial institutions, looking for robo-technology but lacking the knowledge, time, and expertise to build on their own. By blending B2C/BTBTC models and BTB offers they can diversify their sources of income. Subscription fees harvested from long-tail consumers can be volatile, while SaaS services can help to lower earnings volatility.

Third, Robo-Retirement solutions have great potential and can help Robo-Advisors to evolve from single mindedness into more holistic management of financial well-being. It is easier to disrupt by capturing an existing need rather than creating new ones. The impeding retirement crisis coupled with the generational shift of wealth towards younger generations will provide this opportunity. More than US$ 30 trillion are about to change hands in an environment where retirement insecurity is due to sharpen, which will prompt taxable investors with compelling needs for advanced financial planning.

In fact, FinTech Robo-Advisors are already signing strategic alliances with platforms, asset managers, and banks, aware that their price advantage might not last long. Yet, incumbents serve a greater breadth of personal needs which provides the right fuel to run Goal Based Investing engines.

5.7 CONCLUSIONS: CLIENTS TAKE CENTRE STAGE, AT LAST

Robo-Advisors are changing the way investment decision-making operates with taxable investors. They are disrupting established wealth management businesses by unveiling the asymmetry of information of traditional offers. However, today's transformation is not solely driven by technology: tighter regulation and new client behaviour might be dominant forces operating under the crustal plate of the wealth management industry. In such an evolving digital world financial advice is due to become:

- less product-driven, more client-centric;
- less myopic-trading, more long-term portfolio-making;
- less volume-driven, more added-value focused;
- less cost opaque, more fee-only transparent;
- less asset management (e.g., benchmarking), more wealth management (e.g., advice on holistic financial well-being).

Goal Based Investing is the investment philosophy that corresponds to all these changes. Gamification is a way to simplify the challenges of creating solutions for holistic well-being.

This takes us directly to the last part of our book.

PART Three

Goal Based Investing is the Spirit of the Industry

CHAPTER 6

The Principles of Goal Based Investing: Personalize the Investment Experience

"Imagine how much harder physics would be if electrons had feelings!"
—Richard Feynman (1918–1988)

This chapter focuses on Goal Based Investing, which is the long-term game changer in the process of transformation of the wealth management industry. The principles of this client-centric approach are discussed, starting from its foundations: the theory of motivation and prospect theory. The recognition of personal values, multiple investment goals, multiple priorities, multiple time horizons, and multiple risk profiles allows us to identify the fundamental building blocks of added-value, competitive, and personalized investment experiences. Goal Based Investing should be the rationale behind any strategy of digital wealth management and Robo-Advice 2.0.

6.1 INTRODUCTION

The spirit of the wealth management industry is to provide families and individuals with consistent and up-to-date insights, reasoning, and advice to make wiser and more informed financial decisions about investments, liabilities, and possibly the management of real assets. Any financial investment entails a level of risk, whether a full capital loss or a lower than expected return, which advisors are required to identify and possibly measure. Compared to the boom years of the post-war economy in the US, when Modern Portfolio Theory was initially formulated, investment products have become more complex and leveraged, while markets have exhibited unprecedented levels of volatility and risk contagion among regions and asset classes.

This has posed a significant challenge to both advisors and portfolio managers to discuss investment opportunities with taxable investors, not just for the short but also for the long term. Financial advisors cannot be expected to be mathematicians, thus demanding robust yet intuitive digital tools to support their risk management queries (e.g., Robo-4-Advisors). Experts in quantitative finance, instead, cannot solve mathematically all unknowns related to the dynamics of investment returns. No investment algorithm can be programmed to describe with certainty the potential dynamics of financial markets, and measure and master investment uncertainty in a timely fashion. However, investment managers have historically tended to rely too optimistically on the robustness of pricing and trading models, as was made clear by the default of Lehman Brothers or Long Term Capital Management. A fundamental misconception seems quite often to affect the investment behaviour of many professionals: that risk and uncertainty are interchangeable terms, although they are in fact not the same thing. Risk refers to the lack of knowledge about what is going to happen next, but we know what the distribution of such a potential event looks like. When tossing a coin, we are aware that such a "heads or tails" game is governed by well-known probabilities. Uncertainty instead refers to the lack of knowledge about what is going to happen next, but where we do not know what the possible distribution of such an outcome looks like. When forecasting asset prices we "estimate" the shape of probability distributions but we do not know them ex-ante with certainty. Therefore, algorithms are always refined approximations and cannot model the dynamics of asset prices with probabilistic precision, even though some rules or laws can be found to govern well-known problems in physics. A gravitational force can be measured and replicated under varying assumptions, so that an unmanned spaceship can be propelled to reach Mars with great exactitude. Instead, the dynamics of financial markets cannot be framed mathematically once and for all: there seems to be far more uncertainty than risk walking down Wall Street. This explains why portfolio modelling is only a starting point in investment decision-making and needs to be complemented by other pieces of information, to facilitate a well balanced and informative investment journey.

Why bother? Because portfolio modelling is at the core of Robo-Advisors and client-centric financial advice, and although essential to the risk management of personal investments, it does not solve all the challenges related to the management of financial uncertainty merely by the automation of portfolio rebalancing. Portfolio modelling is essential to clear the table of the wealth management discussion from the appraisal of potential risks and returns that can be reasonably measured. Thus, it will give way to further conversations about what is uncertain (e.g., stress tests or market views) and feature meaningful what-if analysis about how financial decisions (e.g., sell in a downturn), personal or market events (e.g., unexpected need of cash) can hinder the achievement of financial goals. Modern technology allows us to gamify conversations about quantitative trade-off on digital tools, to become the heart and soul of competitive and added-value investment relationships. Since this book is about FinTech innovation in wealth management, we explain the reasons why a technological revolution would be incomplete without concomitant innovation in the methods of finance.

> *"How should wealth managers change their approach to finance, so that technology fosters greater fairness, transparency and personalization of investment decision-making?"*

Modern risk/return measurement owes its methods to physics, although physics and economics are very different disciplines. To quote Nobel prize winner Richard Feynman in his speech at the Caltech graduation ceremony, right after the October 1987 market crash, imagine how much harder physics would be if electrons had feelings! The mismanagement of the emotional relevance in economics is one of the main causes of individuals' tendency to buy high and sell low, hindering trading strategies that seemed to be robust ex-ante. Financial markets and private investors are not governed by rules or law, but are dominated by self-interest, greed, and fear. Therefore, respond to the emotions of the emotionally exuberant or over-conservative.

John Coates (2013) has provided an insightful point of view about the biological sources of emotional trading, leading to market bubbles or crashes, and has discussed what happens to the levels of hormones in people's bodies when they are engaged in risk-taking activities. Coates has recognized that human behaviour follows a biological pattern and the subsequent interaction among people is one of the strongest forces to affect the fate of financial markets. This clearly happens at the macro level, dominated by the play of corporations, political agendas, tax legislation, market regulation, and international flows of liquidity. But it also happens at the micro level, made up of periodic conversations between advisors and their clients, or being part of a do-it-yourself interaction with a Robo-Advisor. The greatest innovation in finance and technology would be to embed elements of investment psychology and cognition within advisory workflows, and recognize the implications of emotions, ambitions, and fears as part of the investment decision-making process. In essence, the investors' goals and their personality should take centre stage, as opposed to traditional approaches which focus primarily on the dynamics of markets and benchmarks.

As simple as it sounds, this change in perspective is not proof against relevant hurdles, because "it does change everything" in most wealth management practices, as described in Brunel (2015). The wealth management industry is traditionally shaped around a mechanism of "product-driven" distribution, while such a change would require the adoption of a "portfolio-driven and client-centric" advisory model. However, widespread revision of market regulation, born out of the ashes of the Global Financial Crisis, demands higher levels of transparency on costs, risks, and incentives. The tightening of the compliance framework significantly increases the costs of red tape for wealth management firms, as well as smaller financial advisors, favouring *de facto* scalable fee-only businesses versus traditional distribution models. The resulting need to reward the advisory relationship with more added value gives lifeblood to the projects of digitalization, and highlights the urgency of creating more emotional and engaging investment experiences. There is nothing more engaging than discussing portfolio construction and investment performance in the light of personal goals, as opposed to market dynamics, and depicting graphically the chances of achieving a desired financial ambition, which in turns translates into a higher probability of attaining personal goals. Individual ambitions and fears, and the "estimated" probabilities attached to their goals, are the main focus in a Goal Based Investing process and replace the traditional conversation about tracking the risks and expected returns of benchmarks, to remind us that financial markets are dominated by risks and uncertainty which need to be reviewed against personal targets. As Chhabra (2015) put it: "If the markets don't really care about you, as surely they do not, then why should you spend all your time and effort trying to beat them?"

Rudimentary attempts to embrace GBI principles lie behind the curtains of the digital interfaces of many Robo-Advisors. They were created as effective on-boarding mechanisms capable of attracting customers on the basis of their simplicity, coolness, and convenience. They are attempting to keep investors explicitly engaged through the cycle, by focusing on long-term performance toward final goals as opposed to idiosyncratic discussions. They are offering their services at discount prices, fostering a realignment of the asymmetry of information. But in essence, they have showcased the feasibility of institutionalizing the private banking relationship, by inviting clients to invest in portfolios which are more clearly labelled around thematics (e.g., retirement, education, housing) displaying different purposes and investment horizons. This is a relevant discontinuity from the DotCom propositions of the 1990s, since the business focus is shifting from idiosyncratic investing (e.g., stock picking) towards passively managed portfolios for long-term targets. However, current Robo-Advisors cannot yet compare to best GBI practices, as articulated by the work of Brunel (2015). Notwithstanding, the need to differentiate further within the wealth management and FinTech ecosystems, and move beyond initially price-driven and single minded business models, will push innovators to innovate further. This time around innovation will not be "disruptive" but "sustaining", since the final battle will be fought by means of competitive and added-value GBI Gamification.

"Today's investment is tomorrow's competitive growth."

Investors have a difficult time ahead: the student loans crisis is impending in the US, as is the retirement crisis globally. Therefore, understanding the interaction between these risks and uncertainty is of the utmost strategic relevance for financial institutions and FinTech entrepreneurs, because their capability to provide adequate answers and solutions could ultimately decide the fate of their businesses, as opposed to the search for digital excellence alone which can be easily commoditized. While already transforming, wealth managers need to understand the competitive landscape in 2020 to succeed as winners instead of becoming laggards.

This chapter provides an understanding of what Goal Based Investing means to help build long-term strategies for the development of digital offers. It features some highlights of academic theory, presents the building blocks of the approach, discusses the aspects of a consistent elicitation of goals and risk profiles, and showcases the advantages of GBI graphical reporting. Discerning the essence of Goal Based Investing supports our advocacy for a renewed interpretation of portfolio theory, based on probabilistic scenario simulations, and prepares the terrain to discuss the insights of investment Gamification.

6.2 FOUNDATIONS OF GOAL BASED INVESTING

Goal Based Investing is about informing individuals on how to invest to achieve personal goals and invite them to dedicate time to a balanced elicitation of personal ambitions and fears, as opposed to an attempt to tame the markets and formulate investment policies based solely on tracking of benchmarks. Traditional wealth management practices have been primarily driven by an asset management perspective. This perspective focuses on reporting ex-post performance and expected returns of preferred indices or benchmarks to influence asset allocations, without embedding consistently the elicitation of the many ambitions individuals formulate when investing their money, their varying level of risk acceptance, the existence of different investment horizons, and liquidity constraints.

So far, three elements have prevented GBI principles from becoming mainstream, despite being fair and valuable. First, technology was not accessible to many financial advisors and family officers to help them institutionalize a GBI-driven investment relationship with intuitive and economically convenient processes. Robo-technology, digital experiences, and Gamification principles are available nowadays to close this gap, as Robo-Advisors have started to demonstrate. Second, individuals are not rational investors and are truly dominated by traits such as greed and fear. They tend to compare themselves quite often to what their peers or other professional investors might have gained in financial markets, instead of pondering the risks involved and the impact on personal goals. The Global Financial Crisis has reduced people's comfort and confidence in tracking the performance of financial markets, and has affected the reputation of traditional firms as sources of investment advice. This has ignited widespread discussions about the costs and values of active management and idiosyncratic investing, compared to long-term and more passive investment management in the light of personal goals and thematics, as Robo-Advisors have begun to show. Third, Modern Portfolio Theory has dominated portfolio management ever since its first Mean-Variance formulation in the early 1950s. MPT is a model of portfolio diversification, which assumes the existence of a unique efficient frontier which identifies optimal portfolio allocations for given levels of return or risk targets over a single investment horizon. However, individuals exhibit multiple goals, multiple risk attitudes, and multiple investment horizons. Human beings exhibit biases and references, which make the understanding of how they truly decide more relevant than the modelling of how they should react rationally in principle. Most investors would feel more pain when they lose money than the pleasure they would get when they earn the same amounts. Investors are not consistently risk averse and do not have a global view of their investments, but hold separate mental accounts and are willing to gamble more from some of the accounts than from others. Brunel (2002, 2003, 2015) and Chhabra (2005, 2015) have pioneered the use of mental accounts to shape investment advice around well-defined Goal Based Investing principles.

Yet, most wealth management practices remain confined to MPT-related approaches, notwithstanding the known pitfalls, due to an apparent lack of valuable alternatives. Most likely, a professional tendency to simplify investment decisions to the dynamics of benchmarks, and rely on mainstream theories for compliance purposes, has also played a relevant role. The turning point was the publication of a seminal paper by Das, Markowitz, Scheid and Statman (2010), in which the authors concluded that mental accounts and Mean-Variance optimization are mathematically equivalent, hence resolving an initial criticism that GBI approaches might lead to sub-optimal investing due to the allocation of wealth into separate optimal buckets, instead of single optimal portfolios on a unique efficient frontier. However, a discussion about mathematical optimality or sub-optimality of mental accounts versus a single minded optimization might miss the main added-value and business point of GBI. Traditional portfolio optimization is typically about measurement of the measurable unknowns, not about understanding the impact of uncertainty on portfolio returns and the affordability of personal goals. The true added value of GBI resides in moving the investment discussion from expected returns and volatility towards the probability of achieving or missing an investment goal. The game changer resides in the chance to support a more consistent, intuitive, balanced, and informative wealth management experience with modern and fit-for-purpose quantitative methods, and help to resolve investment biases within a robust risk based framework, more than finalizing a debate on mathematical preferences.

This is why the remainder of this book discusses the opportunity to update portfolio choice beyond classical MPT configurations, and presents the principles of Probabilistic Scenario Optimization (PSO), as in Sironi (2015). GBI frameworks can be strengthened by means of scenario analysis, joint simulation of multiple investment horizons, stress tests, market views over time, and risk management of real products (especially fixed income and derivatives). Scenario modelling opens the way for educational Gamification, as a means of helping investors to gauge risk and uncertainty by reconciling ex-ante the potential impact of their decision-making across the short, medium, and long term. If not academia, then digital practice is dictating the relevance of Goal Based Investing at a time when portfolio management is becoming commoditized, within an industry that shifts from product-driven toward portfolio-driven and client-centric models. Wealth managers are asked to showcase added value to their techno-literate clients who are becoming more demanding in terms of personalization, thematics, and transparency.

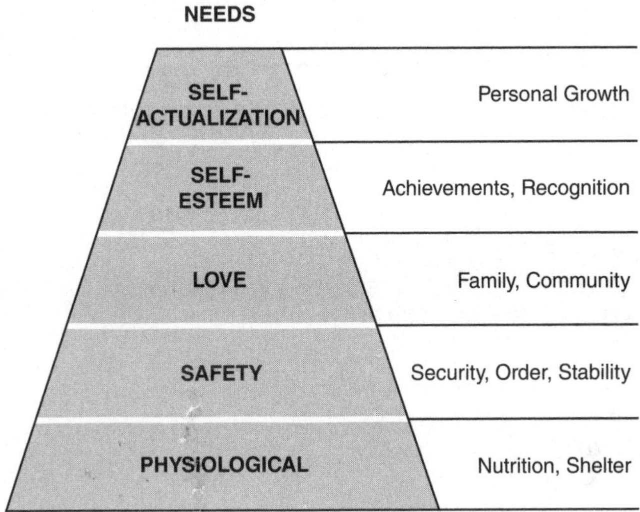

FIGURE 6.1 Maslow's Motivation Pyramid

6.3 ABOUT PERSONAL NEEDS, GOALS, AND RISKS

Abraham H. Maslow (1943) formulated an insightful theory of human motivation which sheds light on the relevance of personal unconscious motivations as opposed to conscious statements, centring upon ultimate goals instead of partial ones, recognizing that humans arrange their preferences in hierarchies of relative predominance so that one need usually rests on the prior satisfaction of another, which is influenced by the field in which an individual reacts, whether in an integrated fashion or as a set of isolated decisions. Although Maslow's theory is about motivation and not behaviour, it is a key starting point for subsequent advances in behavioural finance and Goal Based Investing. Human needs are organized as shown in Figure 6.1:

- **Physiological needs:** which correspond to the physical drives such as food, water, and shelter.
- **Safety needs:** which refer to human preference for safe, orderly, predictable, organized environments in which unexpected things (danger) cannot occur.
- **Love needs:** which indicate the relevance of affectionate relations within a community or in the intimacy of a family.
- **Self-esteem needs:** which emphasize the search for recognition, reputation, or prestige.
- **Self-actualization needs:** which are the desires for self-fulfilment, such as becoming everything that one is capable of becoming.

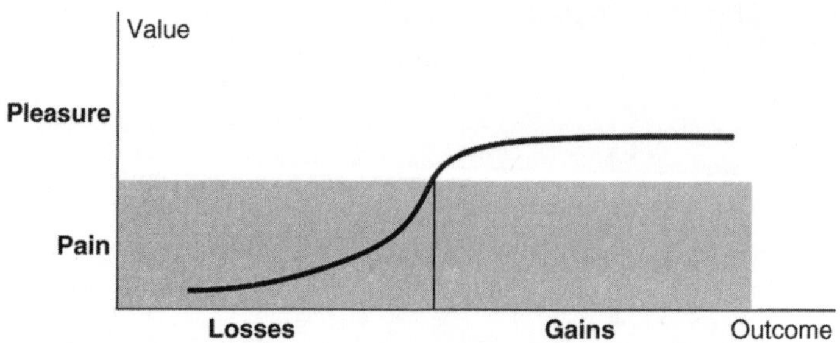

FIGURE 6.2 Prospect theory

Kahneman and Tversky (1979) laid the foundations of prospect theory. They articulated that individuals tend to fear losses more than appreciate gains of the same monetary magnitude (as in Figure 6.2), and therefore make inconsistent decisions with regard to the level of risk aversion. The contradiction in people simultaneously owning an insurance policy (e.g., safety need, low risk) and playing the lottery (self-actualization need, high risk) is well known.

Further advancing from the theory of motivation and prospect theory, Shefrin and Statman (2000) centred their research on the idea that individuals have multiple goals, similar to Maslow's idea that human beings have multiple needs, and that individuals have different risk profiles for each goal, which is reflected in a hierarchy of prepotency. Instead of possessing a global view of their investments, they tend to reason according to separate mental accounts which leads them to accept at once very different gambles.

Brunel's Behavioural Portfolio (2002, 2003, 2015) and Chhabra's Wealth Allocation framework (2005, 2015) have refined the original discussion, by redrawing Maslow's hierarchy as a hierarchy of goals and associated risk profiles, as shown in Figures 6.3 and 6.4.

Taking from Chhabra (2005, 2015), investors have multiple goals which can be organized in three main buckets:

- **Essential goals:** which would ideally correspond to physiological and safety needs, and refer to building a safety net that protects from a variety of risks such as mitigating the loss of employment, severe health issues, lack of retirement income, children's and spouses' well-being in case of investor's death.
- **Important goals:** which refer to the achievement of personal and family stability such as a constant or growing standard of living within a community, nation, or group of peers.
- **Aspirational goals:** which entail pursuing personal dreams and aspirations, such as philanthropic giving, significantly expanding a business, or achieving a unicorn type of investment return. By pursuing such goals, individuals might be prepared to face significant investment losses as a price for the highly aspirational potential.

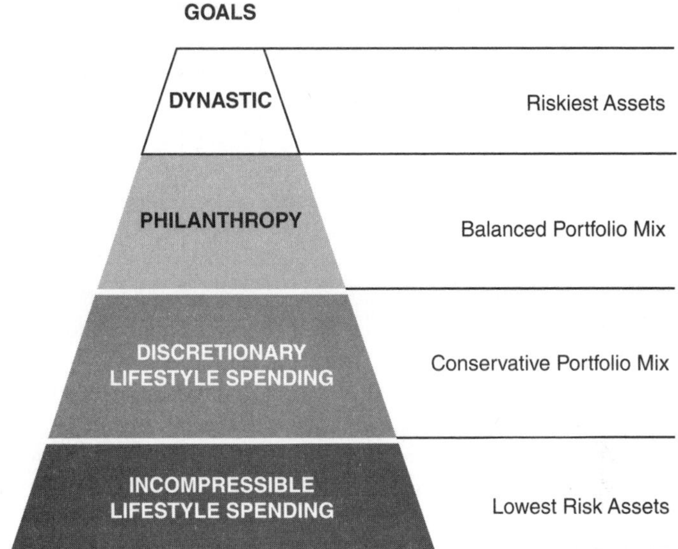

FIGURE 6.3 Brunel's Behavioural Portfolio

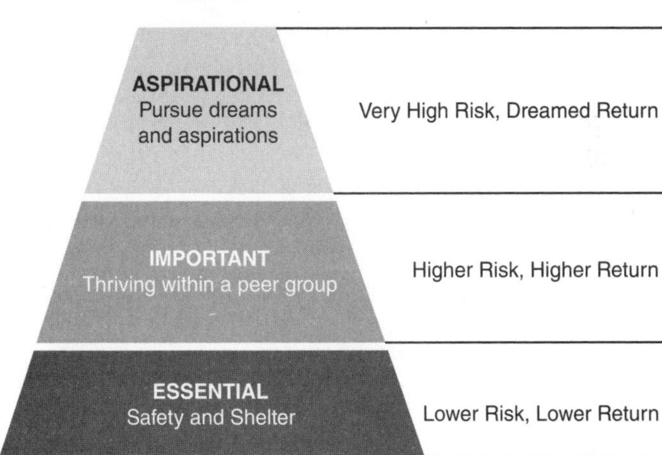

FIGURE 6.4 Chhabra's Wealth Allocation Framework

Within a Goal Based Investing framework, investors are required to take their time, isolate their personal goals, prioritize them, project potential cashflows over time to identify most appropriate investment horizons, aggregate them into fewer buckets and figure out how much money should be invested today or periodically contributed into an adequate set of suitable investment policies, which would be designed to enhance the probability of fulfilling all goals. Thus, people need to make sure that aspirational investment returns do not jeopardise the fulfilment of more essential ambitions. The key rationale would be to insulate investors' essential goals from the dynamics of the financial markets, while granting them enough probability to achieve important targets and allowing for the opportunity to achieve aspirations.

Since each goal represents a different return ambition, they can be remapped into different types of risks:

- **Personal risks:** which require protection against falling short of fundamental needs, such as granting access to essential cashflows and avoiding a dramatic decrease in the standard of living.
- **Market risks:** which arise from investments required to improve personal finances in order to keep up with increases in the cost of living as well as comparative increases in average wealth due to financial market trends. Market risks are therefore linked to the dynamics of financial markets and no cost-effective portfolio can fully diversify them away.
- **Aspirational risks:** which stem from idiosyncratic risks aimed at fostering wealth mobility, hence entailing the potential to generate substantial capital gains or losses.

To go back to investment practice, the elicitation of goal buckets and the definition of the corresponding risk profiles constitute the building blocks of an informative and transparent set of investment policies which can be implemented separately, reviewed individually, optimized and stress tested holistically, should theory and financial engines permit:

- **Safety portfolios:** consisting of protective assets (e.g., liquidity, primary residence, retirement savings, short-term and highly rated Fixed Income or Inflation Linked).
- **Market portfolios:** with the objective of stability in the long term (e.g., bonds, stocks, mutual funds, alternative assets ... all with the most balanced and adequate mix).
- **Aspirational portfolios:** to target aspirational goals (e.g., family-owned businesses, private equity ownership).

Table 6.1 summarizes the mapping between buckets, risk typologies, and model asset allocations.

The fact that personal goals can be organized into hierarchical categories is common knowledge nowadays, and this approach is useful for the majority of investors, irrespective of their worth. Clearly, affluent and UHNW would place different personal emphasis on goals like "saving for retirement" and "philanthropy". A consistent periodic assessment of personal preferences, ambitions, fears, and current investments

TABLE 6.1 Goal buckets, risk profiles, and model portfolios

Bucket	Risk	Portfolio
Essential	Personal	Safety
Important	Market	Market
Aspirational	Aspirational	Aspirational

(e.g., share of wallet) would be essential for any financial advisor or Robo-Advisor to provide holistic Goal Based Investing advice. However, financial advisors might not be able to collect all relevant information from their clients and gain a full picture of their assets and liabilities. Investors might not be used to dedicating enough time and discussing goals, time horizons, and risk appetite due to insufficient financial literacy as well as entrenched investment habits. Furthermore, Robo-Advisors are currently focused on very simplistic engagement mechanisms based on easy-to-complete self-assessment questionnaires and limited investment proposals (e.g., thematic portfolios), although a great effort in the area of design has been made to avoid potential clients' perception of being pigeon-holed. Yet, most of them already organize their engagement model around thematics, hence potential goals. Although this seems to be the right first step, going forward it might not be enough to fulfil the growing demand for personalization stemming from a very competitive marketplace which serves Generation X and especially Millennials. The fight for personalization is not just a problem of technology, such as Big Data analytics to personalize news and insights on a digital tablet, nor can it be confined to the creation of a smarter and cognitive dialogue before investments are made. The fight for personalization will be fought by providing seemingly unique financial advice and related investment policies, which correspond to actual goals and comply with individual core values with regard to personal, social, or environmental issues.

The innovative search for successful and competitive investment experiences needs to be affordable as well, and allow streamlining of all aspects of pre-investment compliance without missing out on the chance to garner cognitive insights on clients and generate asset allocations which correspond to the right thematics, align with desired impact investing, and preserve essential goals from the fate of aspirational bets. Leading FinTechs, platforms, or financial institutions will be those capable of using technology to support the procedural hurdles of Goal Based Investing, and making efficient use of robo-technology, Big Data analytics, cognitive computing, innovative quantitative finance, and digital Gamification to create a compliant and relevant engagement. All these aspects will be discussed in the remainder of this book.

6.4 GOAL BASED INVESTING PROCESS

GBI principles can become the competitive skeleton of a digital transformation based on affordable workflows, the backbones of which are cognitive computing, deep learning, Big Data analytics, social media insights, and scenario analysis. The generation of an added-value investment experience requires the building of an informative dialogue whose outcome is a personalized and compliant investment policy that matches individuals' values and goals. GBI workflows designed to engage individuals and let them invest consciously into relevant thematics (i.e., sub-investment policies or model portfolios) do not need to be very different between family offices, Digital-Advisors (i.e., Robo-4-Advisors) and Robo-Advisors. The workflow can be institutionalized and unbundled into five assessment steps, as shown in Figure 6.5, which enhance the compulsory Know Your Customer (KYC) processes and contribute to the final investment allocation.

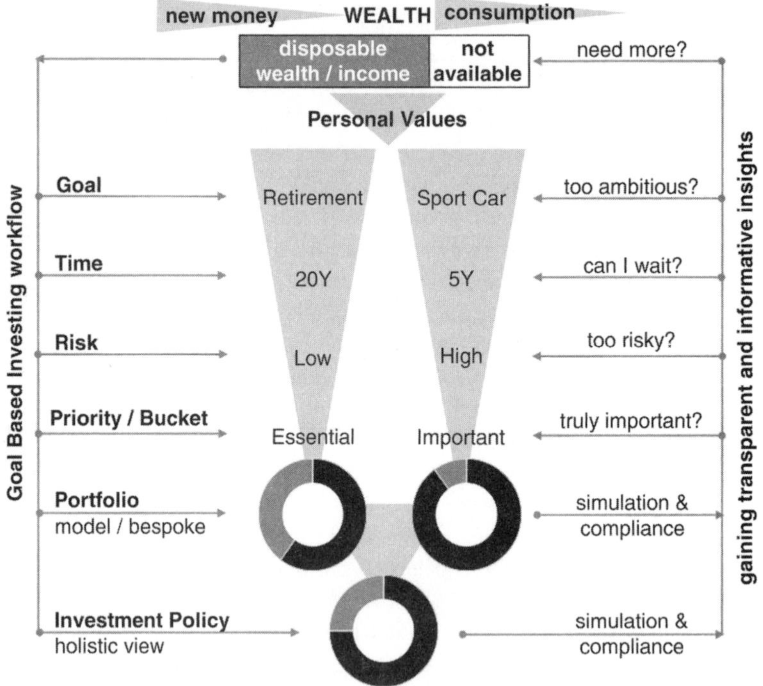

FIGURE 6.5 GBI workflow

- **Personal values:** which identify personal beliefs and sensitivities, to facilitate the personalization around specific thematics or impact investment opportunities.
- **Goals:** which are the needs behind any investment portfolio, and are ultimately formulated as a percentage total return, a target portfolio value, or a required income stream (e.g., post-retirement income or de-cumulation).
- **Time horizons:** which qualify the minimum/maximum holding periods for the sub-investment policies (e.g., short, medium, long, or generational transfer).
- **Risk tolerances:** which assign to each goal the most coherent risk limit (e.g., maximum shortfall probability).
- **Goal priority:** to organize each goal within the most coherent risk bucket (e.g., essential, important, aspirational).

The GBI engagement model is fairly streamlined but must allow for a recursive revision of every decision-making step. It is therefore essential that the financial engine dedicated to supporting portfolio construction allows for interactive what-if analysis, in order to qualify and quantify the impact of any preference and investment decision on potential future outcomes.

6.5 WHAT CHANGES IN PORTFOLIO MODELLING

Setting aside for a moment the relevance of personal values, Goal Based Investing approaches attempt to personalize the investment experience by identifying optimal portfolios which comply with four postulates, that is:

- taxable investors have multiple goals,
- exhibiting different priorities,
- which target multiple time horizons,
- all potentially characterized by different risk tolerances.

Thematic labels have been showcased by many Robo-Advisors and are useful to organize investment goals and prioritize them within risk buckets. Goals can be assigned a quantitative target in terms of desired asset value (or total return percentage) within a time frame, which is also conditional on the initial invested amount and any periodical contribution. Defining optimal portfolios for each goal, in the presence of money in-flows and out-flows, might not be trivial for most financial engines which rely upon classical MPT assumptions. Clearly, given a model portfolio the more an investor contributes, the higher the chances of achieving higher portfolio values over time. But how much is potentially due to the evolution of financial markets and how much would be a function of in-flows? Given that disposable wealth is constrained, is there a way to understand ex-ante what would be the best balance? Moreover, long-term investing might require an even more complex design than myopic bets. First of all, although target date is distant, risk constraints need to be verified periodically: we have learned in Chhabra (2005) that the journey matters as much as the destination. Secondly, more complex goals aimed at supporting post-retirement needs (e.g., income targets or de-cumulation out-flows) require quantification of the investment objective in terms of affordability to buy an annuity or conform to a certain pattern of wealth de-cumulation, which is not always a trivial quantitative task.

Traditional portfolio construction techniques do not aways seem to be fit for purpose. Therefore, further financial innovation is required to exploit all the added-value advances that GBI approaches seek to deliver. In particular, compared to traditional MPT, it seems relevant to:

- **change the risk measure** and introduce the probability of achieving or missing a goal as key criteria;
- embed a **multi period verification** mechanism within portfolio modelling, to account for the relevance of the journey as well as the destination;
- facilitate the simulation of **real products** within portfolio modelling, to enhance risk management, add valuable insights, and improve compliance;
- simulate and optimize portfolios by accounting for **in-flows and out-flows**;
- allow the expression of investment goals as the **affordability** of future investment decisions (e.g., buying an annuity at retirement).

Das, Markowitz, Scheid and Statman (2010), Chhabra (2005, 2015), and Brunel (2002, 2003, 2015) have provided the academic imprimatur for the advocacy of the change of risk measure, indicating the probability of achieving a goal (hence its complement, the probability of missing a goal) as the key objective of GBI portfolio construction. Sironi (2015) has attempted to address the remaining issues with Probabilistic Scenario Optimization (PSO), and opened the GBI framework to the use of risk factor simulation and scenario analysis, which are building blocks of an investment Gamification based on sound quantitative methods. While traditional approaches typically define portfolio risk as the volatility of potential returns, or a quantile of their distribution (e.g., Value at Risk), what seems relevant for individuals is not the minimization of an arbitrary level of loss but the minimization of the probability of missing their financial goals. Since most solutions assume normality of portfolio returns, in a Mean-Variance framework we can look at the simplified normal distribution of potential portfolio returns and identify the probability associated with any level of return ambition, as shown in Figure 6.6. The optimal portfolio would correspond to the asset allocation that would produce at a given time horizon the highest target return, with a minimum required probability of success.

Further distancing from the Mean-Variance limitations, Sironi (2015) has allowed definition of the optimal portfolio module as the asset allocation that exhibits the highest probability of success (hence minimum probability of failure) along the time horizon, constrained by a multi-period risk limit that can be expressed with quantile measurement (e.g., VaR profile over time), as shown in Figure 6.7.

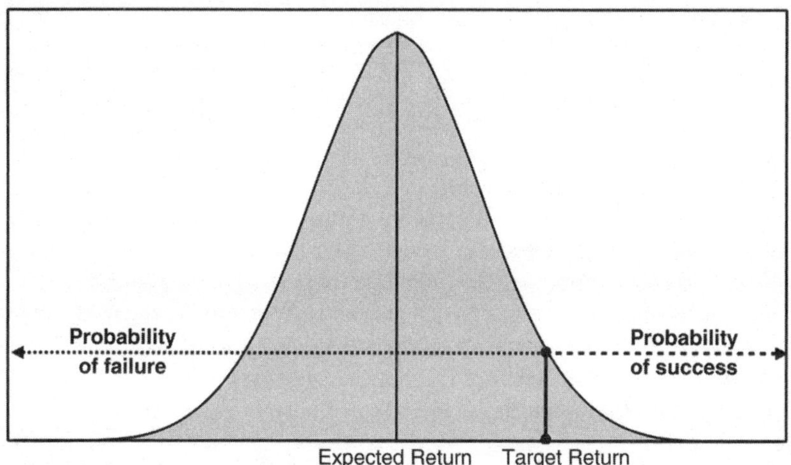

FIGURE 6.6 Probability of a given return on a normal distribution

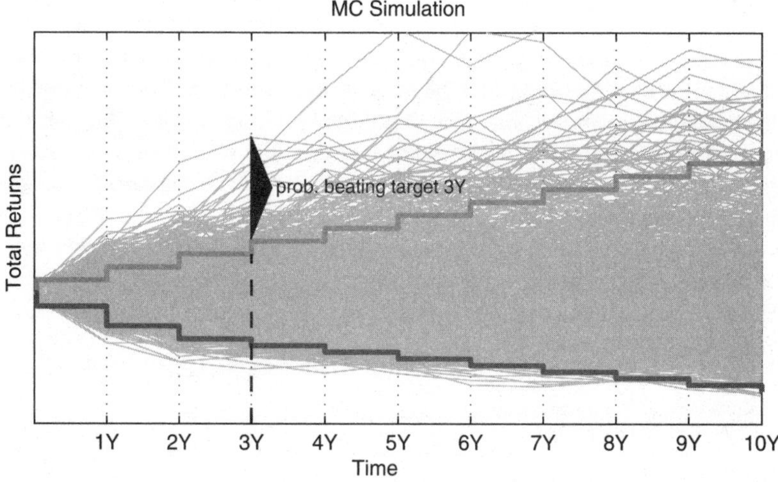

FIGURE 6.7 Monte Carlo simulation and return target

The quantitative aspects of these optimization approaches will be drafted in the next chapter. What follows is a revision of the five assessment steps of the GBI workflow, as shown in Figure 6.5: personal values, goals, priorities, time horizons, and risk tolerances.

6.6 PERSONAL VALUES

Understanding ethical and behavioural thought processes of clients provides valuable insights about their emotional preferences to drive the whole GBI workflow efficiently. Yet, advisors are not psychologists, time is money, and individuals can be reluctant to engage in an investment conversation centred on personal ethics. What clients care about, what they believe is worth doing, and what makes them passionate are all answers to probing questions which modern analytics can help to collect and transform into an engaging interaction. This is not just relevant as a first step with a prospect, but provides emotional suggestions to keep clients engaged over time, allowing for less formal conversations about reassessment of goals and leading to risk-effective portfolio rebalancing. How can technology enhance the understanding of personal values? With particular regard to Millennials, their use of social media can provide Robo-Advisors and Robo-4-Advisors with a relevant source of information about personal interests and values which can be scanned by analytics and deep learning engines to provide insights about the personal relevance of environmental issues, sensitivity to tobacco usage, sports preferences, interests about social issues in certain regions more than others, etc. This would allow the positioning of a filtered set of thematics (e.g., travel, children's education, tobacco-free investments), which can be referred to when making investment proposals and increase the level of customization within an institutionalized framework. Moreover, smart digital tools could allow association of the right emotional images to thematic portfolios, which would be perceived as more aligned with personal preferences and values. For example, a Digital-Advisor could start to ascertain an aspirational bucket by showing on a digital tool the image of a Ferrari instead of a vineyard in Tuscany, should social media analytics report that the client has been frequently tweeting about Formula One races as opposed to the latest wine rankings by Robert Parker. Moreover, cognitive computing can be used by Robo-Advisors to create insightful yet automated conversations based on personality insights, whenever human interaction is not part of the assessment process.

6.7 GOAL ELICITATION

Shefrin and Statman (2000) stated that individuals have multiple goals and different risk profiles for each goal (e.g. lottery versus insurance, pension versus IPO). Goal elicitation, prioritization, and mapping to buckets are the essence of Goal Based Investing. Paradoxically, Brunel (2015) reminded us that the major challenge with a client-centric process is that clients are required to remain engaged through the whole workflow, while traditional approaches obviate this need since clients are more simply asked to pick a portfolio out of a risk-tolerant selection and be satisfied with the outcome. Therefore, creating the right engagement and experience seems to be a winning factor to help financial advisors in guiding their clients through the steps of the process, in particular in visualizing goals which are far into the future. That most of us will depend on retirement money is obvious, although many individuals fail to understand how relevant it is to start saving and investing for retirement while still being young professionals. Moreover, it might not be easy to discern how much retirement income will be deemed enough by looking far into the future, and hence set a meaningful quantitative target.

Digital tools can help to create life planning experiences with graphical representations of personal needs and most likely timelines (Figure 6.8), so that the process of goal elicitation can become more interactive and possibly gamified. Every goal can be conceived as a personal scenario into the future: having US$ 20,000 more in 5 years, or buying an annuity to yield US$ 1,000 every month after retirement. Since financial goals can be represented as thresholds which can be achieved conditional to specific scenarios, financial engines operating on scenario analysis seem to provide greater added value because they allow simulation of future statements of wealth performance over time and visualization of their effects on potential goals. This helps to understand if portfolios are exposed to excessive risk, but also if goals are too ambitious or insufficient given the implications of the passage of time on compounded returns and the likelihood of economic realization. The winning factor lies in the availability of a financial engine capable of marking to future investment products and strategies, which decouples product performance and the evolution of the underlying variables (i.e., risk factors). Brunel (2015) also advocates that asset allocations based on risk factors rather than asset classes become the norm, as it allows

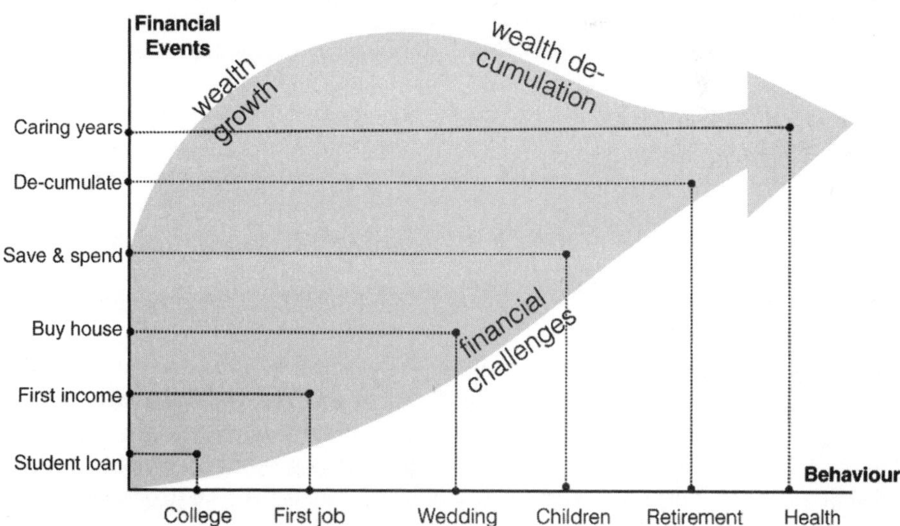

FIGURE 6.8 Example of timeline for life events

for a more differentiated and finer analysis and management of the risks involved in a portfolio and, we would add, the affordability of personal ambitions.

6.8 GOAL PRIORITY

Shefrin and Statman (2000) state that individuals have multiple goals and have different risk profiles for each goal. The scope of Goal Based Investing resides in allowing individuals to invest with purpose, and hence associate more clearly financial needs and the investments that best fit. At the same time, Goal Based Investing seeks to ensure that invested amounts and investment compositions are thoroughly crafted so that lower priority goals can never jeopardize essential ones. Building a hierarchy of prepotency is truly valuable as it allows account to be taken of emotions during a market downturn, because it can provide a clear picture of the risks undertaken and the potential still open to reach personal financial ambitions.

6.9 TIME HORIZONS

The essence of any financial decision-making process is always about the consistent appraisal of three elements: portfolio risk, personal ambition, and investment horizon. Yet, although much time is devoted to the understanding of risk and return, not enough is usually dedicated to making sure that the passage of time, which elapses between the present and the realization of desired goals, is properly modelled and represented. Brunel (2015) reminded us that Goal Based Investing enables the establishment of the link between "My Wealth" and "My Life", which means understanding how needs can change over time, how relevant it becomes to anticipate strategies aimed at resolving future funding needs, and that future life is not deterministic but that personal events, decisions, or external factors can influence our minimum requirements, sometimes suddenly.

Investing is therefore a journey, in which private investors should be allowed to travel with the tools and equipment necessary to enjoy the trip, as well as cope with the abrupt changes in the terrain. Goals are meaningful only if minimum and maximum investment horizons are also set to judge their effective realization. As individuals have multiple goals, they clearly have multiple investment horizons, and hence need to discuss investment opportunities across the timeline and through economic cycles. The capacity to absorb losses in the short term for goals whose horizon is set far into the future can be fundamental to avoid the tendency to buy high and sell low, and thus enhance final investment returns. It is therefore paramount to be capable of designing potential scenarios to assess the interrelation between essential, important, and aspirational goals over different time steps. Chhabra (2011) reminded us that the journey matters, as indicated in Figure 6.9. Hence, understanding how different

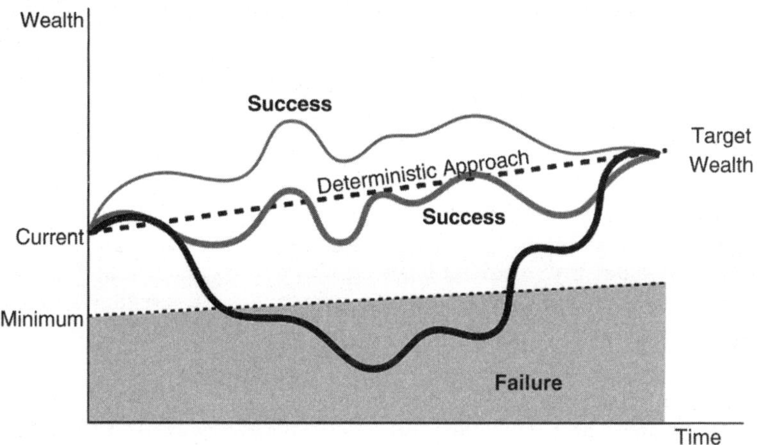

FIGURE 6.9 Time matters

sub-investment policies interact over time is essential to build a holistic view of personal wealth changes.

Yet, classical advice relies upon expected return and variance, which are hardly meaningful indicators of investment risk/return potential for the short term, and clearly not suitable indicators for the medium to long term. This is why Probabilistic Scenario Optimization (PSO) is drafted in the remainder of this book, because only a financial engine built on scenario analysis over time can facilitate ex-ante understanding of the risks that lie ahead and accommodate for stress tests to check the effective robustness of the hierarchy of prepotency to face uncertain events.

6.10 RISK TOLERANCE

The risk profile is the result of a process of investigation aimed at identifying which investments are suitable and adequate for an individual, that is how much risk (e.g., potential losses) a client can tolerate. Post-GFC market regulation has strengthened the relevance of achieving a consistent elicitation of investors' risk profiles, although principles and recommendations are not always aligned internationally. Most strikingly, although risk tolerance is a key hub of the compliance process, regulators have been setting principles more than prescriptive mechanisms, which has favoured the appearance of differing practices among industry participants which have been largely relying upon static paper questionnaires. The effectiveness of the risk assessment, which is part of the on-boarding mechanism of Robo-Advisors, can be significantly improved by using smart technology and become an educational opportunity for investors. Enhancing the compliance framework allows for more suitable and risk adequate investment propositions, hence lowering potential attrition and regulatory costs.

An individual's risk tolerance is a combination of subjective and objective elements, namely risk aversion and risk capacity, both combining to shape an individual's perception of financial risks, hence relevant to a consistent calibration of the GBI workflow. Risk aversion (e.g., pain from losses) is the subjective factor which determines the willingness to take on risks as a result of psychological traits and emotional responses. Risk capacity (e.g., personal wealth) is the objective factor which determines the capability to sustain financial losses of a certain magnitude without jeopardizing essential goals. Clearly, the fact that clients are wealthy yet conservative does not imply that they should be allowed to invest part of their wealth in very risky bets, just because potential losses would not affect their financial well-being. More importantly, knowing individual risk capacities is a relevant factor to mitigate framing biases during the elicitation of risk aversion. According to Klement (2015), risk capacity and risk aversion are closely linked and common practices for risk questionnaires seem to be too weak, as limited or excessively standardized, leading to the underestimation of investors' risk tolerance. Individuals dealing with paper questionnaires react with more vivid emotions when presented with larger loss scenarios than smaller amounts, or abstract figures such as percentage losses. That is, confronting the emotions for a potential loss of US$ 20 for US$ 100 invested would be different than presenting a loss of US$ 2,000 for a US$ 10,000 investment. Therefore, it seems fundamental to shape investigations about risk aversion by framing the dialogue with due knowledge of individuals' risk capacity and actual investment amounts.

What drives and influences the forging of personal levels of risk tolerance? Klement and Miranda (2012) seem to indicate that genetic imprints, past experiences, and the environment we interact with are key drivers. We have already mentioned the work of Coates (2013) on the biology of risk, linking traders' exuberance and over-conservativeness to the level of hormones, hence genetic predisposition. Yet, asking for a DNA test does not seem to be a viable step of a risk assessment phase. Instead, looking at life experiences and the interaction with the community in which a client lives and works seems to be more easily accessible and convenient. It is well known that after a market downturn investors are less willing to invest in stocks than after the recovery of a prolonged bull market, because the memory of a recent loss is still vivid and influences emotional reactions to investing. However, past experiences are also very relevant, such as the social conditions and market environments during formative years, which can affect individuals as well as whole generations. Brown, Ivković, Smith and Weisbenner (2008) have also discussed the relevance of peers and communities, presenting insightful evidence about their potential influence on the amount of risky asset ownership: it seems that moving an individual to a community characterized by higher stock participation would consequently increase the acceptance of stock investing.

Financial advisors and regulators might still fall short in recognizing that investors tend to exhibit multiple risk tolerances, and failing to account for this might lead to very inefficient dialogues and asset allocations. GBI workflows allow us to calibrate risk tolerance to individual goals. Yet, all goals and underlying risks can be aggregated in a hierarchy of prepotency to fit single minded compliance. Smart financial engines would allow the embedding of a hierarchy of risk tolerances in the construction of portfolios, similarly to what financial institutions would do when allocating risk capital to trading desks. No sub-investment policy of higher risk and ambition should hinder the probability of reaching essential goals when investments are jointly simulated over time, acting as a global limit to the holistic asset allocation. However, the risk definition needs to be enhanced. Classical approaches define the risk profile starting from the traditional MPT assumption that investors are willing to take on extra risk only if they can garner higher anticipated returns to compensate them for higher risk, thus identifying which investments are suitable and adequate. Nothing is necessarily said about the consistency between the levels of risk and declared ambition. Goal Based Investing innovates on the definition of risk, and introduces the probability of missing a target as a key driver of the asset allocation process. This allows definition of an asset allocation as adequate, not solely against a personal risk tolerance, but also against a specific goal and helps gauge how reasonable investors' expectations are compared to the risks they are willing to on-board.

How can technology enhance the elicitation of the risk profile? First, digital tools allow us to move out of tick-box questionnaires and create smart dialogues between personal financial advisors or Robo-Advisors and respective customers. Questions and answers could be generated in the most inbiased fashion to avoid framing, placed in the context of an individual's life cycle (e.g., Generation X), experiences, and communities. Second, social media analytics could provide valuable insights into cognitive dialogues by contextualizing questions and answers to the profession, location, religion, and ethical considerations of customers. Third, quantitative finance enhances risk measurement and assessing the probability of achieving or missing goals across different buckets and time horizons without losing consistency.

6.11 REPORTING GOAL-CENTRIC PERFORMANCE

So far, we have discussed the advantages of Goal Based Investing to enhance a transparent intuitiveness in financial decision-making, by mapping thematic portfolios to investors' emotional needs. Since this client-centric approach is far more demanding than a traditional brokerage or advisory model, it is relevant to make clients feel comfortable during the whole process, which does not seem to be affordable without institutionalizing the workflow. GBI innovates the way individuals make investment decisions, by themselves or by consulting with personal financial advisors or Robo-Advisors, because portfolio propositions become aligned to the way people think about their money, more than the way institutions think about creating MPT portfolios. Clearly, GBI also innovates the way investment performance is

TABLE 6.2 Example of performance report

Products	Weights	Mkt Value	Quarter	YtD	from Start
ETF 10	5.00%	5.00	+2.00%	+10.00%	+20.00%
ETF 20	15.00%	15.00	−20.00%	+11.00%	+7.00%
ETF 30	10.00%	10.00	−17.00%	+5.00%	+4.00%
Fund 100	10.00%	10.00	+3.00%	+10.00%	−15.00%
Bond 1000	30.00%	30.00	+1.00%	+3.00%	+3.00%
Bond 2000	30.00%	30.00	+1.00%	+1.00%	+3.00%
Total	**100.00%**	**100.00**	**−3.70%**	**+1.85%**	**+2.75%**

reported, because the focus moves away from quarterly analysis of benchmarks and asset returns, toward the establishment of a progress-to-goal dialogue. Implementing client-centric policies and reporting goal-centric performance can be time consuming and too expensive without appropriate technology, which involves a revision of back-ends and front-ends of established firms. Robo-Advisors have a competitive advantage, as they can construct their system architectures without much reliance on the past. We have learned that clients seem to care about mental accounts, but custodians have no knowledge of this and tax authorities care about the asset's ownership irrespective of the investing purpose (setting aside tax advantaged retirement savings). Therefore, the following complexities need to be addressed:

- Money is not always deposited with a single entity and financial advisors require tools of account aggregation and disaggregation to map holdings or part thereof to individual goals and buckets.
- Discussing the aggregated investment policy is still relevant, due to compliance and tax reasons related to regulatory risk tolerance and investment rebalancing. Regulators and tax authorities do not have mental accounts.
- Clients are used to traditional reporting, which makes it advantageous to provide a reconciliation of both views.

Therefore, robo-solutions need to solve the tasks of aggregation and disaggregation across buckets and goals, as depicted in Figure 6.10.

We can assume a simplified example in which US$ 100 are invested in six products at the same start date. Table 6.3 exemplifies a traditional report (numbers and quantities are only indicative).

Table 6.3 exemplifies instead a GBI report for an investor having two goals with different investment horizons.

The probability of reaching a goal is a function of the performance so far, as well as the remaining potential evolution of the financial market variables affecting the price of any security over time. It is also a powerful way to isolate those portfolios, hence clients, among the thousands, hundreds of thousands, or millions whose asset

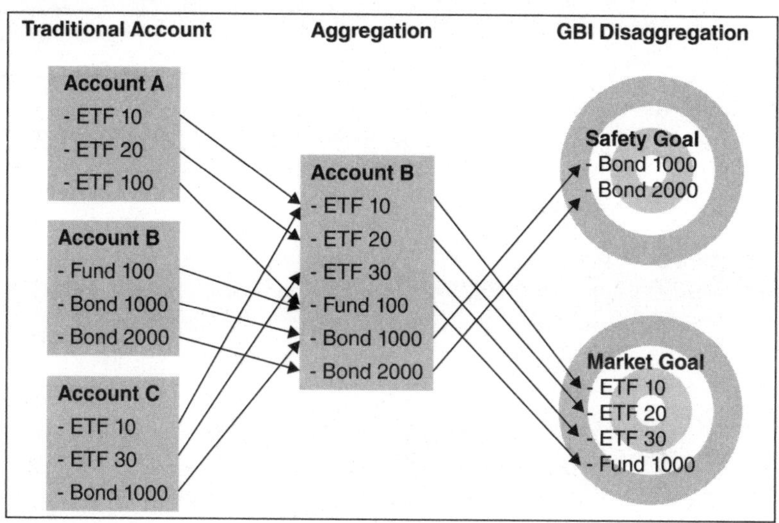

FIGURE 6.10 Managing and reporting GBI performance

TABLE 6.3 Example of GBI performance report

Products	Weights	Mkt Value	Goal 7Y	from Start	Prob.
Bond 1000	50.00%	30.00		+3.00%	
Bond 2000	50.00%	30.00		+3.00%	
Total	**100.00%**	**100.00**	**+10.00%**	**+3.00%**	**98%**
Products	**Weights**	**Mkt Value**	**Goal 4Y**	**from Start**	**Prob.**
ETF 10	12.50%	5.00		+20.00%	
ETF 20	37.50%	15.00		+7.00%	
ETF 30	25.00%	10.00		+4.00%	
Fund 100	25.00%	10.00		−15.00%	
Total	**100.00%**	**100.00**	**+20.00%**	**+2.37%**	**55%**

allocation does not seem sufficiently robust within a financial planning context. Therefore, alerts can be generated to inform financial advisors about those clients needing more care, while providing an intuitive though quantitative rationale for the rebalancing discussion. Figure 6.11 features a simplified graphical representation of portfolio performance, which depicts intuitively ex-post performance (which is known after disaggregation of asset ownership from the individual goals) and ex-ante performance (which is estimated with a Monte Carlo process).

The remainder of this book describes how to enhance portfolio modelling and make insightful graphical representations of investment performance.

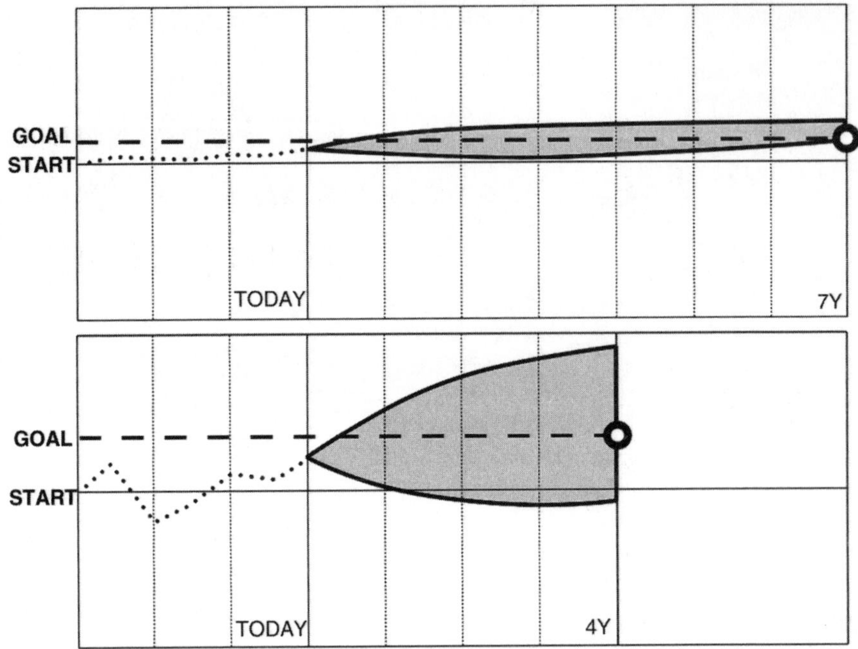

FIGURE 6.11 Managing and reporting GBI performance

6.12 CONCLUSIONS

Goal Based Investing is a game changer in wealth management as it moves the advisory dialogue from the advisor-centric approaches of MPT based portfolio construction to the hierarchy of client-centric goals. Financial innovation can be supported by technological innovation to institutionalize the GBI approach and make it affordable to financial advisors, as well as entertaining and engaging for final investors. The rest of this book will discuss portfolio construction, without delving too much into its mathematics, simply to highlight the main assumptions underling Modern Portfolio Theory and its current implementations by many Robo-Advisors and financial institutions (e.g., Mean-Variance, Black-Litterman), the modifications already mentioned to comply with GBI principles, and further advances (e.g., PSO) to build a more robust risk based simulation framework, which strengthens GBI added value and allows for scenario analysis and Gamification.

CHAPTER 7

The Investment Journey: From Model Asset Allocations to Goal Based Operational Portfolios

"Creating a new theory is not like destroying an old barn and erecting a skyscraper in its place. It is rather like climbing a mountain, gaining new and wider views, discovering unexpected connections between our starting points and its rich environment. But the point from which we started out still exists and can be seen, although it appears smaller and forms a tiny part of our broad view gained by the mastery of the obstacles on our adventurous way up."

—Albert Einstein (1879–1955)

While FinTechs largely position themselves as revolutionaries in personal finance, they often rely upon simplified portfolio construction methods which seem incomplete with regard to modern risk-management techniques and scenario analysis, and can ultimately lead to inconsistent graphical representation of the potential performance of model portfolios. Therefore, this chapter outlines key aspects of portfolio modelling, which shape the investment propositions of many Robo-Advisors. First, Mean-Variance and Black-Litterman optimizations are drafted, being the most commonly used techniques to construct model portfolios for private wealth. Second, a recent modification to Mean-Variance is introduced, as a relevant development to address client-centric solutions. Thus, Probabilistic Scenario Optimization is discussed, as a risk-based framework whose building blocks and principles can lead Robo-Advisors 2.0 to achieve advanced Goal Based Investing and insightful Gamification.

7.1 INTRODUCTION

J. M. Keynes had already imagined central bankers as orthodontists, intervening with humble fiscal and monetary policy to optimize the dynamics of the economy at large:

"If economists could manage to get themselves thought of as a humble, competent people, on a level with dentists, that would be splendid." As Campbell and Viceira (2002) indicated, it is now common wisdom that dentists also pursue the goal of advising on oral hygiene, rather than simply intervening once the pain becomes unbearable. Similarly, investors will be given the tools and the means to rebalance investments with an ex-ante view of the potential drawbacks and opportunities, which is the essence of proactive wealth management. Empowering taxable investors to take transparent care of their own investments, directly or indirectly via the professional work of personal financial advisors or Robo-Advisors, responds to the industry imperative to comply with post-GFC market regulation (e.g., transparency, suitability, and adequacy principles), and should be a key driver to judge the effectiveness of any project of banking digitalization. Individuals need to be better informed *a priori*, and attain an adequate level of understanding of the risks and uncertainty they are exposed to by investing in financial securities or seemingly diversified portfolios. Nowadays, reliance on the fate of financial markets is not an individual's choice but a *de facto* necessity: governments require that citizens become more directly responsible for taking care of their retirement savings which are allocated to market portfolios (e.g., Australian superannuation funds). This exposes the essential goals of tax payers to the appropriateness and soundness of investment decisions. Understanding how investment risks and returns can unfold becomes a social imperative, not just in the short term (myopic trading) but also in the long term (capital protection).

> *"How is the wealth management industry coping with these changes? Are the methods used to describe risk and return sufficiently transparent, intuitive, and robust? Are the techniques adopted to create asset allocations in line with the need to personalize the investment experience around individuals' goals and constraints?"*

Unfortunately, the industry seems to be fairly undifferentiated with respect to the methods and solutions of portfolio construction. Although Robo-Advisors have taken the lead in the innovation race, transforming the investment management industry with intuitive reporting and captive engagement models, they still rely upon traditional portfolio theory, even though it might be too restrictive to build and explain long-term optimal asset allocations, particularly if multiple investment horizons and goals have to be accounted for.

Modern Portfolio Theory (MPT) relies on the work of Harry Markowitz (1952), whose Mean-Variance proposition combines the basic objectives of investing: maximizing expected return or minimizing risk. This leads to an efficient frontier that indicates the set of portfolios with the best combination of risk/return characteristics given the stated objectives. It has its limitations. The time dependent total return dynamics of many securities (e.g., fixed income and derivatives) cannot be conveniently embedded. Although Robo-Advisors typically rely upon linearized ETF based portfolios, traditional wealth managers might not have such a narrow focus on investment catalogues. Most importantly, adequate modelling of fixed income securities and liabilities would be disregarded, although fundamental to build a competitive GBI proposition. This is a strong limitation for Robo-Advisors, should they want to evolve into holistic solutions for private wealth, and encompass financial planning featuring cumulation and de-cumulation patterns on top of the price stochasticity of model portfolios. Moreover, the Mean-Variance efficient frontier often indicates extreme portfolio weights, forcing portfolio managers to impose tighter constraints to their algorithms and closely guide the construction of model portfolios. Investors' goals do not explicitly enter the framework, but only expected returns and standard deviations of market securities. Professional investors might believe they possess asymmetrical information about these securities, but tweaking the estimates of their expected returns might lead to unstable or over-sensitive portfolio weights.

Black and Litterman (1992) proposed an elegant approach to alleviate some of these limitations. They indicated the positive weights stemming from the market equilibrium as the initial reference portfolio, and thus combined return expectations with wealth managers' subjective views of the market and led to a more reasonable, less extreme, and less sensitive portfolio weighting scheme. Although this approach seems to be popular among Robo-Advisors, it cannot address some relevant risk management challenges: the resulting strategic asset allocation relies on the dynamics of estimated benchmarks or linear products, while embedding professional views in consistent formats is not always convenient. Once more, investors' goals must enter the framework.

Most optimization engines generate model portfolios with a combination of linear products (e.g., ETFs), which Robo-Advisors propose to on-boarding clients directly. Traditional wealth managers, instead, rely on equally simplified rules of thumb to assess the trade-off between investment risks and returns, but refer to a broader set of securities that their clients can invest in. Therefore, they might need to handle a larger diversity of operational portfolios, which do not always reconcile to model portfolios directly (e.g., strategic asset allocations). The developments in portfolio theory outlined in this chapter explain how to move out of this impasse, avoid excessive simplification in product/portfolio selection, yet attain a streamlined and informative set of diversified and personalized investment propositions. The provision of more intuitive and consistent information about potential future states of the world and the simulation of actual investment returns instead of benchmarks – net of commissions, transaction costs, and possibly tax – can contribute to reconciling tactical and strategic portfolio allocations for digital wealth managers. Robo-Advisors might not yet feel compelled to discuss the gap between strategic and operational asset allocations, since they typically on-board new money directly to model portfolios, but the need to differentiate and solve graphically complex and more personalized investment decisions (e.g., retirement planning) requires all market participants to discuss the long-term competitive advantage of embedding enhanced techniques of portfolio construction and simulation.

"Can the optimal portfolio be the same for long-term investors and short-term players? Is cash a risk-free heaven when looking at longer investment horizons, in which reinvestment occurs at today's unknown real interest rates? Can wealth managers provide long-term capital protection but also yield returns stemming from tactical opportunities, in such a way that investments are always optimal during the multi-period?"

Post-GFC market regulation demands more risk transparency and stimulates a revision of portfolio modelling towards clearer risk based approaches, based on actual products, actual investors' preferences, and actual investment goals over the life cycle. A new interpretation of portfolio theory is therefore emerging to realign more consistently investments and goals, which is the essence of Goal Based Investing.

First, a seminal paper by Das, Markowitz, Scheid and Statman (2010) allowed us to make a significant step forward, by demonstrating that working with mental accounts is mathematically equivalent to the original Mean-Variance proposition if the risk measure is replaced by the probability of falling short of an investment goal.

Second, in Sironi (2015) we show that Probabilistic Scenario Optimization (PSO) enriches GBI optimization by modelling scenarios over time and opening up a larger set of investment goals (e.g., retirement income) and insightful Gamification. By simulating the potential evolution of market variables (e.g., inflation expectations, commodity prices, term structures of interest rates) and repricing the investment products on the basis of future world situations, wealth managers can estimate potential total returns of actual investments and liabilities over the life cycle, and access the information hidden in the probability densities of actual products. Thus, they can verify whether a given set of an individual's constraints complies with the simulated total return space of portfolios, by measuring on demand the probability of achieving or under-performing a defined investment goal. In essence, the probability measure becomes the key variable of the min/max objective function used in GBI portfolio modelling, being the key information to discuss where portfolio performance lies against a stated goal, at any point in time of the investment journey.

Final investors and industry commentators should become more aware of the intrinsic advantages and pitfalls of the financial engines operating in the shadow of digital interfaces, which showcase captive user experiences. They should learn to criticize or demand more from Robo-Advisors and digital Wealth Managers when it comes to the graphical representation of future goals and potential portfolio performance. This chapter features a mathematical discussion of portfolio theory. Some formalization is needed, but will be kept to a minimum because this is not a book of quantitative finance, but a discussion about wealth management transformation. However, establishing the key features of the optimization models would be valuable for all readers because the design of these quantitative engines, which operate in the back-office of Robo-Advisors, affects the quality and robustness of their investment propositions and has a strategic impact on all front-end representations. These modelling choices can restrict or enhance the competitiveness of digital architectures in adapting to further changes in business models, client requests, and market conditions.

7.2 MAIN TRAITS OF MODERN PORTFOLIO THEORY

Markowitz's brilliant intuition, based on simple Mean-Variance assumptions, has inspired portfolio theory since the early 1950s. It is now widely held that optimal portfolios need to solve a quantification problem, related to the maximization of a measure for central tendency (expected return) or the minimization of a measure of risk (variance). The generation of all possible combinations of the securities inside a portfolio, whose expected return and variance is derived from the estimates of the individual securities (often asset classes), allows us to plot the set of all attainable portfolios on the cartesian plane with the x-axis being the standard deviation (for convenience) and the y-axis the expected return, bounded by the so-called efficient frontier as in Figure 7.1: for any given level of risk, there is no other portfolio with a higher expected return, or vice versa. Knowing the efficient frontier, investors can choose a portfolio that corresponds to their risk/return target, which is the asset allocation that corresponds to the tangent point between the efficient frontier and the utility function.

Over the course of time, the original formulation has been further enriched by mathematical refinements that introduced more advanced risk measures (e.g., semi-variance, tracking error, expected shortfall), but the theory is not proof against weaknesses. The model does show excessive sensitivity to the historical calibration of the statistical parameters such as expected returns, covariances, and variances. Variance is a convenient but imperfect risk measure. However, computational convenience has contributed to making Mean-Variance an appealing reference at numerous firms. Notwithstanding the limitations, what certainly stays in portfolio theory about Markowitz's formulation is the explanation of the importance of portfolio diversification: model portfolios are a combination of risky and non-risky assets, so that a

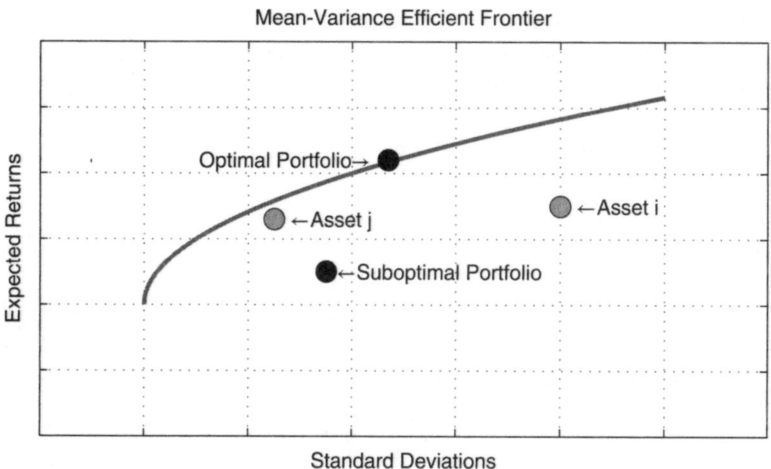

FIGURE 7.1 Efficient frontier

suitable return is sought while risk is diversified away, as much as possible. How does portfolio diversification work and what is the efficient frontier?

7.2.1 Asset diversification and efficient frontier

We assume that there are only two assets (namely 1 and 2) in the investment universe, which are denominated in the same currency. It follows that portfolio value V_U is indicated by:

$$V_U = V_1 w_1 + V_2 w_2 \tag{7.1}$$

The weights w_1 and w_2 add up to 1: extreme portfolios can be constructed by investing 100% into either of the two given assets and zero in the other.

Mean-Variance is based on the estimate of portfolio expected returns and standard deviations, which are a combination of the expected returns, standard deviations, and pairwise correlations of any potential security in the portfolio. Expected returns need to be explicitly estimated for any given time horizon T: moving from a short-term representation to a long-term representation typically requires re-estimation of all parameters by using a different length of time series. It is conveniently assumed that the longer the time series, the more "appropriate" the estimation of long-term expected returns, as a way to capture long-term trends in the market variables or mean reversion. Therefore, portfolio expected return $\overline{R}_U$ is indicated by:

$$\overline{R}_U = \overline{R}_1 w_1 + \overline{R}_2 w_2 \tag{7.2}$$

While the portfolio return is a linear combination of the returns of the underlying assets, weighted by the relative w_1 and w_2 contributions to total portfolio value V_U, standard deviation ρ_U is not a linear measure but a quadratic function of asset volatility. Therefore, given the volatility and the portfolio weight of each asset, portfolio risk is typically indicated by:

$$\sigma_U = \sqrt{\sigma_1^2 w_1^2 + \sigma_2^2 w_2^2 + 2 w_1 w_2 \text{cov}_{(1,2)}} \tag{7.3}$$

where

$$\rho_{(1,2)} = \frac{\text{cov}_{(1,2)}}{\sigma_1 \sigma_2} \tag{7.4}$$

One can therefore express the above equation as follows:

$$\sigma_U = \sqrt{\sigma_1^2 w_1^2 + \sigma_2^2 w_2^2 + 2 w_1 w_2 \sigma_1 \sigma_2 \rho_{(1,2)}} \tag{7.5}$$

The correlation coefficient ρ can take a maximum value of +1 (i.e., the two assets are perfectly correlated, that is they move in perfect unison) and a minimum of −1 (i.e., they are perfectly negatively correlated, that is their movement is the opposite of the other). To understand how portfolio risk is affected by the correlation assumptions, we can investigate the extreme cases when correlation is equal to −1, is null, or equal to +1.

If pairwise correlation is equal to +1, the covariance between the two assets will equal the product of the two volatilities: the volatility of the portfolio becomes a linear combination of the volatility of the underlying assets. Hence, plotting the relationship between portfolio returns and portfolio risk on the cartesian plane, for any given combination of asset weights, would lead to a straight line.

$$\begin{aligned}\sigma_U &= \sqrt{\sigma_1^2 w_1^2 + \sigma_2^2 w_2^2 + 2w_1 w_2 \sigma_1 \sigma_2} \\ &= \sqrt{(\sigma_1 w_1 + \sigma_2 w_2)^2} \\ &= \sigma_1 w_1 + \sigma_2 w_2\end{aligned} \tag{7.6}$$

Similarly, where correlation equals −1, one can plot on the cartesian plane a segment that, although monotonic in the expected returns, can solve portfolio returns for two different attainable but equally likely asset allocations, that depend on the portfolio relevance of the exposure of each of the two assets against the other:

$$\begin{aligned}\sigma_U &= \sqrt{\sigma_1^2 w_1^2 + \sigma_2^2 w_2^2 - 2w_{1,0} w_2 \sigma_1 \sigma_2} \\ &= \sqrt{(\sigma_1 w_1 - \sigma_2 w_2)^2} \\ &= |\sigma_1 w_1 - \sigma_2 w_2|\end{aligned} \tag{7.7}$$

When instead correlation equals 0, then the resulting function is not linear:

$$\sigma_U = \sqrt{\sigma_1^2 w_1^2 + \sigma_2^2 w_2^2} \tag{7.8}$$

Figure 7.2 shows a numerical example in which the expected returns are respectively $\overline{R}_1 = 14\%$ and $\overline{R}_2 = 4\%$, while the standard deviations are $\rho_1 = 8\%$ and $\rho_2 = 3\%$. The plotted line representing the risk/return characteristics of a potential model portfolio invested in the two assets is contained in the space identified by the extreme cases, in which the assets are perfectly correlated and perfectly uncorrelated, for any value of $\rho_{(1,2)}$ between −1 and +1.

Hence, for any given estimate of $\rho_{(1,2)}$ and any given portfolio composition (w_1,w_2), one can identify the minimum return portfolio, the maximum return portfolio, and the minimum variance portfolio. As $\rho_{(1,2)}$ is also an input in the optimization exercise, the objective function would solve for a suitable combination of portfolio

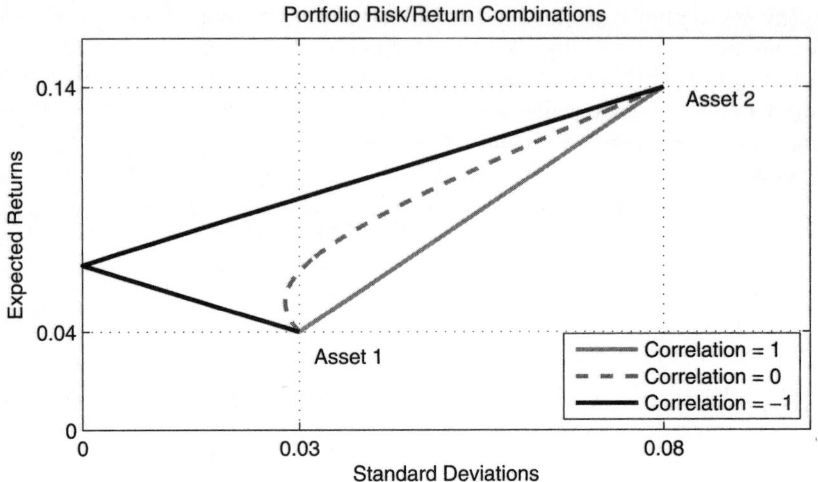

FIGURE 7.2 Diversification (two assets)

weights. When the number of assets is greater than two, as in the three assets case represented in Figure 7.3, then pairwise correlations are indicated by a variance-covariance matrix. Allocation constraints are usually specified for the various asset classes: the problem becomes multi-dimensional and mathematically advanced routines are required to identify the global minimum/maximum of the optimization objective function (e.g., minimization of standard deviation). The best mix of risky

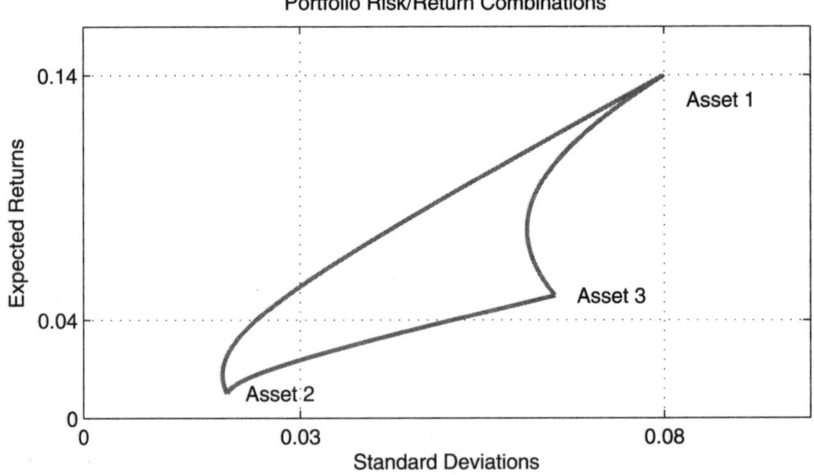

FIGURE 7.3 Diversification (three assets)

assets for every maximum level of expected return is a curve, indicated as the efficient frontier.

7.2.2 The Mean-Variance model portfolio

Finding the model portfolio, for a given investor and a given set of constraints, requires us to move along the efficient frontier to attain the desired expected return with the minimum portfolio variance. Therefore, the efficient frontier is the "collection" of all portfolios that optimize the objective function, under the same set of constraints but for different target expected returns. We assume that the universe U of the available securities is made up of any j_{th} securities. Each security has been associated with an expected return $\overline{R}_j$ corresponding to the mean return of the historical distribution or a subjective opinion of the portfolio manager, while w_j denotes each security's fair value exposure within the portfolio. As $w_{j,}$ can equal zero, we can identify a portfolio with the notation U as a set of all securities that an individual can invest or not invest in. We can also assume that σ_j is the volatility of the j_{th} security, while $\text{cov}_{(i,j)}$ refers to the covariance between the returns of any pair of securities (often asset classes).

The classical case identifying the model portfolio by setting a target return and finding the optimal asset allocation to minimize portfolio variance takes the form of a quadratic programming problem:

$$\min_{w} \sigma_U^2 = \min_{w} \left\{ \sum_{j \in U} w_j^2 \sigma_j^2 + \sum_{j \in U} \sum_{i \in U, j \neq i} w_j w_i \text{cov}_{(i,j)} \right\} \tag{7.9}$$

subject to:

- the resulting portfolio yields at least a target $\overline{R}_U^*$

$$\sum_{j \in U} \overline{R}_j w_j \geq \overline{R}_U^* \tag{7.10}$$

- all portfolio weights sum to 1:

$$\sum_{j \in U} w_j = 1 \tag{7.11}$$

- short selling is typically not allowed:

$$w_j \geq 0 \tag{7.12}$$

Varying $\overline{R}_U^*$ between the return of the minimum variance portfolio and the return of the maximum variance portfolio indicates the efficient frontier, as in Figure 7.1.

The optimization engine is usually guided by setting constraints on any amount that can be invested in a particular asset class or currency A⊂U so that the exposure in A is no more than a certain b percentage of V_U:

$$\sum_{j \in A} w_j \leq b \tag{7.13}$$

Once the efficient frontier is built, Robo-Advisors may break it into segments and identify levels of risk and expected return that map onto client profiles as defined in the on-boarding mechanism. Hence, a model portfolio is presented to the investor as a personalized and optimally chosen investment recommendation.

7.2.3 Final remarks about Mean-Variance

Mean-Variance is the simplest and most convenient optimization case, which limits the representation of real securities to linear products or their equivalent asset class estimates (e.g., indices), deals with a single investment horizon at a time, restricts to the use of expected returns as a measure of future profitability, and plugs in variance as a measure of risk. Although more recent techniques allow enhancing the risk estimate with more refined measures, such as tracking error volatility or expected tail losses, wealth managers would still be asked to optimize portfolios separately for different time horizons, and reduce the conversation about investment ambitions to the expected return instead of discussing the probability of achieving personal goals through the market cycle.

7.3 MAIN TRAITS OF BLACK-LITTERMAN

In 1992 Fischer Black and Robert Litterman published their work on asset allocation which they had built internally at Goldman Sachs. Their Bayesian portfolio construction model has three elements of originality: first, the idea that information about financial returns is asymmetrical and can be divided into long-term market equilibrium (e.g., CAPM) and short-term investors' views; second, that both sets of information are uncertain and can be described by means of probability distributions; third, that a complete set of expected excess returns can be estimated by combining professional views with the market equilibrium, which becomes the new input of the revised Mean-Variance model. Litterman and He (1999) observed that the approach overcomes the tendency of classical theory to generate non-tradable portfolios that are extreme and over-sensitive to the updates of the parameters. Therefore, the Black-Litterman model has been adopted by quite a few Robo-Advisors as it relates to the possibility of embedding subjective beliefs of expected returns and guides the construction of model portfolios accordingly, yet uses quantitative methods. Black-Litterman is quite an elegant model, but shares with Mean-Variance some relevant limitations with regard to reliance on the estimate of expected returns and volatilities, and the need to simplify fixed income securities and derivatives.

The starting point is the identification of the equilibrium market portfolio and the expected excess returns for all assets or indexes which represent the investment universe. The vector of equilibrium expected excess returns does not necessarily need to be observed directly from the time series of the individual assets, as in the original Mean-Variance formulation, but could result from econometric analysis (e.g., CAPM) to feed the so-called reverse optimization which indicates the initial equilibrium market weights, as in Idzorek (2004). Wealth managers can formulate personal views about the expected performance of securities and related confidence levels, modify the initial equilibrium of the expected excess returns, and then re-optimize the objective function to solve for the portfolio weights that reflect the new inputs.

The steps of this approach can be summarized as follows:

- Preparation of the inputs: identification of the investment universe, estimation of excess returns, estimation of historical variances-covariances, estimation of the risk aversion coefficient.
- Reverse optimization: estimation of equilibrium expected excess returns (e.g., CAPM) and indication of the equilibrium market weights by reverse optimization.
- Declaration of wealth managers' beliefs: declaration of professional views about excess returns of the assets, declaration of the confidence level of those views, estimation of the distribution of those views.
- Portfolio optimization: estimation of the posterior distribution of expected excess returns and optimization to indicate the optimal tilted weights.

7.3.1 The equilibrium market portfolio

The starting point is the equilibrium market portfolio (denoted by M) which corresponds to the investment decisions of all market participants. Continuous trading enables the market to adjust towards a long-term equilibrium value where the market weights w_j^M are governed by frictionless price discovery. Equilibrium market weights can be estimated by assessing the capital value of each asset divided by the total capital value of the whole market:

$$w_j^M = \frac{V_j}{V_j^M} \tag{7.14}$$

The initial investment recommendation would be to hold a combination of the risk-free and the market portfolio (e.g., buy each asset in the universe according to the respective capital weights in the market): for any given level of risk no other portfolio can provide higher expected excess return because trading against the market equilibrium would not be valuable. Yet, trying to construct the real market portfolio would be unrealistic, since the number of assets is enormous in the real world. That is why wealth managers might select a representative market index to approximate the initial equilibrium weights of M.

Alternatively, the approach can be initialized by using the CAPM bet to model the expected excess returns of individual asset classes (as in Sharpe (1964) and Lintner (1965)), thus performing reverse optimization to derive the equivalent CAPM weights that represent the initial market equilibrium. The time series of the excess returns of each j_{th} asset with respect to the risk-free r_f are the initial input for the estimation of the CAPM equilibrium, so that:

$$\overline{R}_j^{capm} = \beta_{(j,M)} \overline{R}_M \tag{7.15}$$

in which,

$$\beta_{(j,M)} = \frac{\text{cov}_{(j,M)}}{\sigma_M^2} \tag{7.16}$$

$$\overline{R}_j = \mathrm{E}\left[R_j - r_f\right] \tag{7.17}$$

$$\overline{R}_M = \mathrm{E}\left[R_M - r_f\right] \tag{7.18}$$

The variance-covariance matrix of the excess returns of all assets in the universe is indicated by Σ and allows us to derive the vector of the initial portfolio weights w_j^{capm} by so-called reverse optimization:

$$\overrightarrow{w^{capm}} = (\lambda\Sigma)^{-1} \overrightarrow{\overline{R}^{capm}} \tag{7.19}$$

λ indicates the CAPM risk aversion coefficient (Sharpe ratio) that represents the change in the expected return of the investor's portfolio per unit change in portfolio volatility:

$$\lambda = \frac{\overline{R}_M - r_f}{\sigma_M} \tag{7.20}$$

The implied and reverse optimized excess returns indicate the specified market risk premiums, hence a larger λ implies more excess return per unit of risk adding a positive influence on the level of the estimated excess returns. Under the CAPM theory it is assumed that the idiosyncratic risks of the assets are uncorrelated so that risk can be reduced by diversification. Therefore, the coefficient of the linear regression analysis is assumed to be null since the investor holding the market portfolio will be rewarded only for the systemic risk estimated by $\beta_{(j,M)}$.

7.3.2 Embedding professional views

Wealth managers willing to include their own views in the optimization process would be asked to overwrite the Mean-Variance initial market statistics, thus facing excessive sensitivity on the inputs which would in turn lead to extreme portfolios. Instead, according to Black and Litterman, the views do not directly replace the original historical inputs, but add new information to the exercise as they are combined with the prior expectation of market returns by means of a Bayesian model, thus leading to more stable posterior asset allocations. The information contained in the views can be an absolute or a relative expectation, as investors can express their own beliefs about the performance of an individual asset or the expected performance relative to other investments. Black and Litterman deviate from the assumption of symmetric information (i.e., that all market participants invest or are willing to invest in the same efficient frontier). Robo-Advisors and digital wealth management might believe that they possess superior information compared to the market as a whole and, although accepting asset prices as a starting point to indicate initial optimal weights (prior), they might want their views on short-term dynamics of asset prices to be reflected in the building of the final optimal portfolio (posterior). Their expectations indicate the belief that in the short term, a given asset or set of assets would not converge to the equilibrium but would yield a different return. This belief is uncertain, as it refers to a future state of the world, and it can be described by an expectation and a probability distribution, that is, a view. Therefore, a posterior vector of combined expected excess returns and their related uncertainty is supplied for the final optimization process so that the posterior vector of tilted asset weights is derived: this indicates the optimal portfolio.

The scope of the Black-Litterman approach is to combine the probability density function of initial excess returns with the probability density function of the views, so that the posterior probability density function can be used as an input to the traditional Mean-Variance optimization. The original proposition assumes the distributions are normal, but this assumption could also be relaxed:

$$F_{capm}(R) \sim N\left(\overrightarrow{R}^{capm}; \Sigma\right) \tag{7.21}$$

$$F_{views}(R) \sim N(Q;\Omega) \tag{7.22}$$

Q is a column vector made up of r number of rows, where each row element represents the subjective expected excess return attached to a view and Ω is the confidence interval of the views. The Bayes theorem allows us to construct the combined posterior distribution so that if $\Omega = 0$, then all views are certain so that for all assets specified in the views the return is given by the views themselves; if $\Omega = \infty$, then the views are totally uncertain so that by simplifying the equation becomes $\overrightarrow{\overline{R}^{post}} = \overrightarrow{\overline{R}^{capm}}$.

7.3.3 The Black-Litterman optimal portfolio

Having derived the probability density function of the posterior distribution of the excess returns, one can optimize the Mean-Variance objective function and estimate the posterior "tilted" weights of the assets that indicate the optimal portfolio. This is achieved by solving the following unconstrained maximization problem:

$$\max_{w}\left(w^T\overline{R}_U^{post} - \frac{1}{2}\lambda w^T \Sigma^{post} w\right) \tag{7.23}$$

Similarly to the Mean-Variance case, wealth managers can estimate the Black-Litterman efficient frontier and break it into segments which identify different levels of portfolio expected return and standard deviation. Thus, map investors' risk/return profiles as indicated by the on-boarding mechanism, leading to a "seemingly" personalized and optimally chosen investment proposal.

7.3.4 Final remarks on Black-Litterman

The main advantage of Black-Litterman is to facilitate the embedding of explicit professional subjectivity about future return distributions without creating excessive sensitivity by tilting input parameters. However, portfolio construction is still dependent on a very simplified representation of real investment opportunities which does not allow us to move comfortably outside the convenient zone of ETF investing. This can hinder the simulation and risk management of resulting actual portfolios, and disallow a consistent representation of portfolio sensitivities to market scenarios over time.

7.4 MEAN-VARIANCE AND MENTAL ACCOUNTS

The seminal paper of Das, Markowitz, Scheid and Statman (2010) has been a step forward in portfolio management, and the need to reconcile traditional portfolio theory with the evidence stemming from behavioural finance, that is individuals have mental accounts according to which they make investment decisions, as in Shefrin and Statman (2000). This has facilitated the debate about adopting Goal Based Investing principles as the new normal for personal finance. The Mean-Variance approach features a single efficient frontier which is generated as the best combinations of risky assets to maximize a level of expected return given a volatility target, or vice versa. However, investors seem to be better able to formulate their preferences about expected returns and acceptable risks by discussing individual goals instead of overall portfolios. Moreover, although standard deviation is a simple statistic it does not seem to be an intuitive risk measure, thus its use can lead to opaque decision-making and possibly an inconsistent elicitation of personal risk/return profiles. According to GBI principles, the risk faced by taxable investors can be defined as the probability of not achieving their investment goal. Thus, optimality becomes a set of optimal portfolios which feature the best combination of expected returns and the probability of failing to reach a threshold for each of the mental accounts that map into the different goals. Das, Markowitz, Scheid and Statman indicate that working with mental accounts is mathematically equivalent to Mean-Variance when risk is defined as shortfall probability rather than standard deviation. They also draw an important analytic connection with risk management methods based on quantile measurement, being Value at Risk, a fundamental requirement of most compliance frameworks. The demonstrated mathematical equivalence would allow proponents of classical portfolio theory to advocate the elicitation of goal thresholds and probability of reaching these thresholds for sub-portfolios, rather than eliciting risk/return tolerances by working with risk-aversion coefficients, knowing that mental account optimal portfolios also "lie" on their Mean-Variance efficient frontier. Moreover, wealth managers could aggregate multiple mental account portfolios into an overall allocation, which can also lie on a Mean-Variance efficient frontier. Although it is broadly accepted that the language of probability is more suited to fostering intuitive investment decision-making, much academic debate has been generated in discussing the potential sub-optimality of mental accounts as opposed to the optimization of overall portfolios. The authors also demonstrate that working with mental accounts might be a few basis points less efficient, but yields higher informative value in setting a more transparent and appropriate optimization exercise.

7.4.1 Final remarks on Mean-variance and Mental Accounts

Clearly, this approach is a significant step forward in modelling portfolios for private wealth. Yet, it still suffers from key limitations of Mean-variance and Black-

Litterman: fixed income cannot be conveniently modelled, multi-period goals and their representation cannot be featured, and derivatives cannot become part of portfolio construction. Most of all, since Robo-Advisors invite final investors to stay the course towards the long term, we believe that long-term simulation techniques need to be the basis of portfolio construction and digital representation; hence, Probabilistic Scenario Optimization.

7.5 MAIN TRAITS OF PROBABILISTIC SCENARIO OPTIMIZATION

Probabilistic Scenario Optimization (PSO) is a risk based approach designed to facilitate Goal Based Investing within institutionalized processes of portfolio management, as described in Sironi (2015), to benefit affluent and wealthier clientele without having to over-standardize the offering in terms of securities selection and portfolio allocations. The probabilistic measure of achieving an investment target becomes the key variable of the objective function, which is maximized within a risk constrained exercise over time so that potential losses are also bounded. Portfolio analysis is not restricted to a Mean-Variance representation, but this exhaustive enumeration technique embraces the full valuation of actual securities conditional on stochastic scenarios, which is best practice for market and counterparty risk management: real market variables can be simulated and investments repriced with full revaluation of actual pay-offs, conditional on perturbed market conditions, so that stress tests can also be modelled to assess individual views about financial markets and criticize or validate the results of the theoretical optimums. Full revaluation techniques allow us to close the gap between strategic asset allocations and operational portfolios, since all securities can be simulated jointly and consistently as part of portfolio construction, rebalancing, or analysis. The set of the investors' ambitions and risk tolerances can be represented as threshold lines, and can be graphically plotted on top of the simulated density function of portfolio total returns. Therefore, the appropriateness of investment targets and risk boundaries can be tested on the space of the risk/return simulation. Reinvestment strategies, money inflows and wealth consumption can also be modelled along the time horizon (e.g., de-cumulation during post-retirement years). Thus, Robo-Advisors and digital wealth managers can connect past and future performance into a single representation to drive performance attribution and portfolio rebalancing with intuition.

7.5.1 The PSO process

PSO is a step-by-step process of portfolio filtering and ordering according to a probability measurement criterion, as synthesized in Figure 7.4: the end result is the asset allocation that shows the highest probability of achieving an investment goal, while complying with given allocation constraints and risk limits.

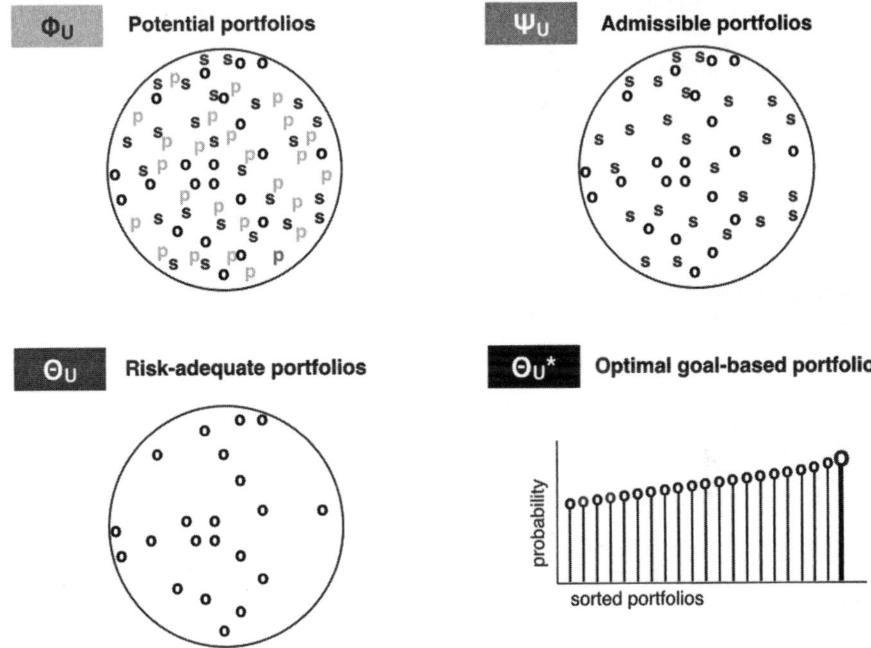

FIGURE 7.4 The PSO process

Advanced risk management methods are required to deal with the estimation of uncertainty about risk/return realizations of actual financial products. Such estimates involve the generation of tens of thousands of stochastic scenarios about the evolution of the market risk factors, that drive fair value pricing of financial securities. The accuracy and meaningfulness of this process are influenced by the quality of the input data and the methodology adopted to simulate the future states of the world for each class of risk factor. The process can be represented by the following steps:

- Definition of the optimization problem: selection of the investment universe, indication of the allocation constraints, declaration of the investment risk/return profile to depict the investment goal and the risk limit.
- Generation of the space of future total returns by simulating real securities over time, conditional on probabilistic scenarios.
- Exhaustive generation of the quasi-random space of the admissible asset allocations and reduction to the risk-adequate set: filtering of all admissible allocations that fulfil the asset allocation constraints and reduction to the set of risk-adequate portfolios with respect to the investor's risk profile.

- Probability measurement and portfolio ranking: optimization of the objective function and graphical representation of the resulting asset allocation and its characteristics.
- Performance measurement and portfolio comparison: investment performance can be tracked over time and the distance to optimality can be measured by computing the residual probability to achieve a target across time.

Exhaustive enumeration techniques are very unrestricted methods and can be applied to any type of investment problem. Hence, Robo-Advisors and traditional wealth managers are provided with a framework that can scale up irrespective of their business focus (e.g., human or unmanned advice), securities universe (e.g., ETF or fixed income), or target clientele (e.g., affluent or UHNW).

7.5.2 The investor's risk and return profile

The process starts with the elicitation of the risk/return profile of the investor, which is a combination of the client's tolerance for risk as well as their declared ambition. Clearly, while risk tolerance is expressed in terms of a statistical moment or a quantile loss of the distribution of potential returns of the final portfolio, the ambition does not refer to any moment or quantile *a priori*. Yet, portfolio construction will allow achievement of the desired combination of risks so that the resulting model portfolio maximizes the probability that the return sought is achieved, that is the one corresponding to the equivalent lowest right-tail quantile. Robo-Advisors and digital wealth managers can gain three benefits:

- encompass both tails of the distribution at once, moving out of the restrictions of the expected return;
- assess convexity of products and portfolios in the joint assessment of risks and returns;
- create a much larger set of goals and risk combinations, which operate on multiple time steps at once.

For example, Sironi (2015) reports in Figure 7.5 the case of a hypothetical moderate investor willing to take an opportunity (hence risk) in the short term, but achieving capital protection in the medium or long term (i.e., a balanced risk/return profile). Figure 7.6 illustrates the hypothetical case of a risk tolerant individual.

The method is sensitive to the setting of the risk tolerance profile as well as the ambition level. Having elicited a risk tolerance, investors can assess how strong their ambition appears when compared to existing market conditions and volatility levels. Given any portfolio that complies with the risk limit, the greater the ambition, the lower the probability of achieving the target. Clearly, different portfolios can exhibit

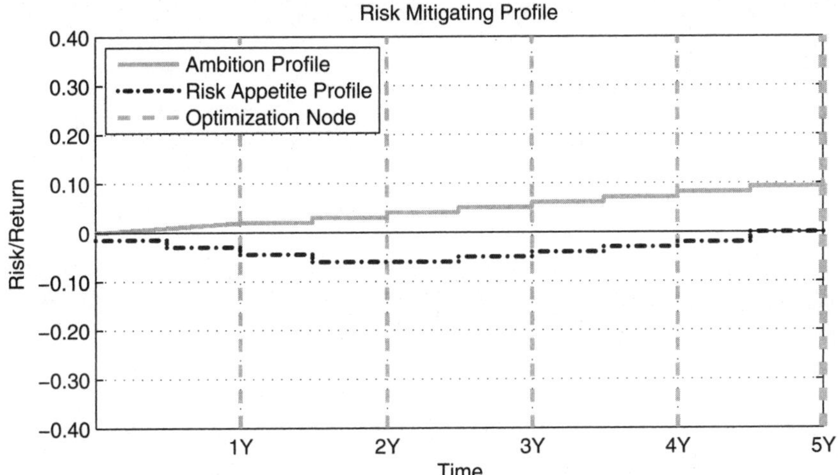

FIGURE 7.5 Example of investor's profile (risk mitigating)

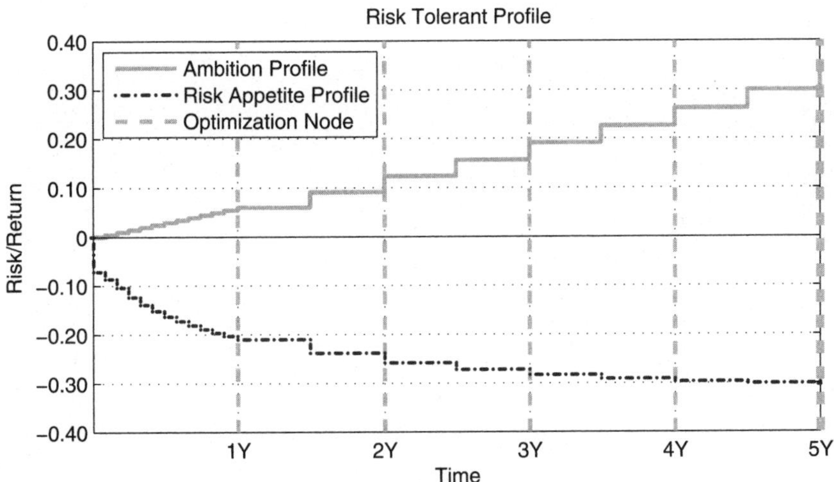

FIGURE 7.6 Example of investor's profile (risk tolerant)

a higher probability of achieving the target, yet comply with the risk constraint. The PSO process allows for multi-period verification of the risk limit, constraints, and objective function. Therefore, the time discretization assumption for compliance checks and rebalancing can be customized to fit wealth managers' or clients' preferences.

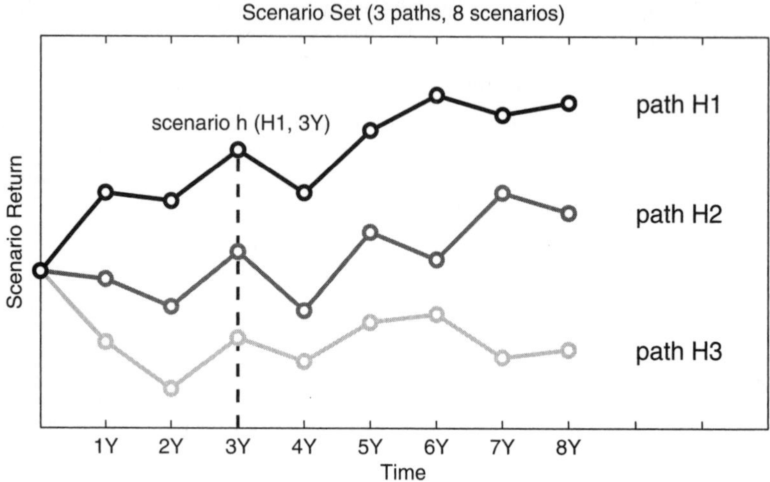

FIGURE 7.7 Example of scenario set

7.5.3 Generation of scenarios and scenario paths

PSO is based upon the full revaluation of security prices, conditional on Monte Carlo scenarios of the underlying risk factors (e.g., inflation expectations, stock prices, term structures of interest rates, credit spreads). In Figure 7.7, a scenario h is a potential state of the world at a particular time, featuring a defined set of risk factors that take on values which are potentially different from their respective evaluation at the beginning of the holding period. A scenario path H is a sequence over time of scenarios $h \in H$ and models the potential evolution of a set of risk factors at any point t along the investment horizon Γ. The set of all scenario paths H is denoted by S.

The measurable uncertainty about the realization of scenario returns is called risk. Conditional on the state of the risk factors in each future scenario, all securities can be repriced and their cashflows tracked to estimate their total return contribution to any portfolio performance over time.

7.5.4 Stochastic simulation of products and portfolios over time

A Monte Carlo simulation can be computed for each of the elements of Ψ_U. This represents the future space of the potential total returns of each portfolio, as a linear combination of the potential total returns of each security conditional on scenarios $h \in H \in S$ and weighted by its portfolio contribution, as in Figure 7.8.

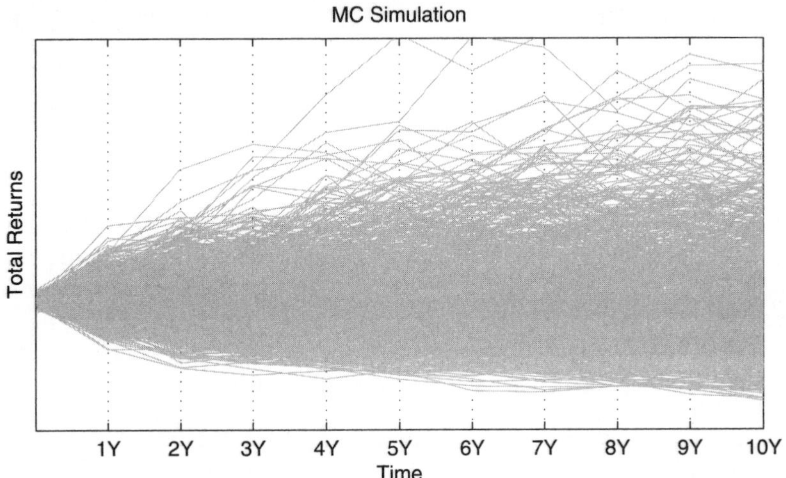

FIGURE 7.8 Example of Monte Carlo simulation

7.5.5 Potential and admissible portfolios: Allocation constraints

The scope of PSO is to investigate the density function of potential returns of all portfolios which are admissible, which means that they comply with a given set of allocation constraints and clients' preferences. $V_{U,H,t}$ is an initial amount of capital to be invested across a universe of opportunities indicated by U, at time t = 0 and conditional on base scenario path H = 0. Φ_U indicates the space of elements identifying all the unrestricted potential portfolio allocations (i.e., the set of the vectors of the potential allocation weights on each of the j assets in the universe). The elements of Φ_U correspond to the individual percentage weights $w_{j,0,0}$ which are constant through scenario paths and time step, since only the fair value of each j security is allowed to change:

$$\Phi_U : V_{U,H,t} = \sum_{j \in U} V_{j,H,t} w_{j,0,0} \tag{7.24}$$

Investments can also be added and money can be withdrawn from existing allocations by modelling potential capital inflows and outflows over time (e.g., income streams, dividends, real estate investments), so that weights can change according to defined rebalancing rules. The amount invested in a particular category A of portfolio U (e.g., asset class, sector, or currency) can be floored (fragmentation limit

a) or capped (concentration limit b), in order to avoid over-concentration or under-representation of specific names, sectors, regions, or currencies:

$$a \leq \sum_{j \in A} \frac{V_{j,0,0} w_{j,0,0}}{V_{U,0,0}} \leq b \tag{7.25}$$

Ψ_U is the final set of admissible portfolios, that is the subset of the unrestricted potential portfolio compositions of Φ_U complying with the allocation constraints. The number of admissible portfolio allocations can grow exponentially with the number of the assets in U and the minuteness of the investment step size, ranging from a few millions to more than one sextillion. Therefore, techniques based on low discrepancy sequences allow us to alleviate the computational burdens without losing accuracy and meaningfulness. In Sironi (2015) we argued for the non-binding adoption of a lexicographical ordering to generate an ordered series of portfolios in an unambiguous canonical order that is similar, but not restricted, to an alphabetical representation (from which the name is taken). Similarly, the explicit list of the ordered asset allocations that make up Ψ_U can be generated by ordering the compositions in such a way that the order associated to each individual asset allocation in the portfolio is preserved throughout the sequence, and is normalized to the unit interval [0,1]. The low discrepancy sequence methods generate a sequence of draws from such a unit interval, in such a way that every draw is far away from the preceding, that is, clustering is avoided (groups of numbers close to each others), and that the draws are maximally avoiding each other, that is larger gaps are avoided. The resulting uniform distribution in the unit interval is used to derive the samples from the ordered universe of the admissible portfolios, that is the final set Ψ_U.

7.5.6 Adequate portfolios: Risk adequacy

Θ_U is the subset of the sampled admissible portfolios in Ψ_U which also comply with the risk limit definition. A risk limit can be imposed as a hard line or as a boundary condition, so that the risk measure (e.g., VaR) of the simulated portfolio is lower than a risk limit or falls within a target bandwidth at preselected time steps, as in Figure 7.9. The risk limit can be idiosyncratic or chosen out of a set of standard profiles that the wealth manager has created ex-ante and underlie the on-boarding risk assessment mechanism.

For a given confidence level 1-α, λ_Γ^L is a risk-limit function over the investment horizon Γ:

$$\lambda_\Gamma^L : \{\lambda_t | t \in \Gamma\} \tag{7.26}$$

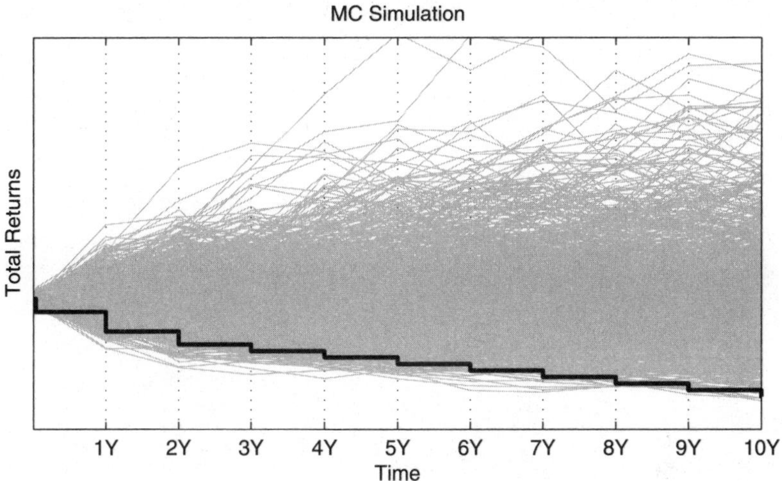

FIGURE 7.9 Example of Monte Carlo simulation

In the case of a hard limit, the probabilistic risk-limit function states a constraint on $\xi\alpha_{U,S,t}$ which is the α-quantile profile of the investor applicable to portfolio returns $R_{U,H,t}$.

$$\xi^{\alpha}_{U,S,t} \leq \lambda^{L}_{t} \forall t \in \Gamma \tag{7.27}$$

This translates into the following statement: the left quantile $\xi^{\alpha}_{U,S,t}$ of the optimal portfolio at any selected time point t, with confidence interval 1-α, shall be contained within the investor's risk appetite λ^{L}_{Γ}.

Clearly, the risk-limit function can operate on a number of reallocation steps which is smaller than the one contained in the simulation framework. Thus, it can incorporate the form of a single point in time constraint. The optimization exercise will check the risk limit only at specified verification points and leave it open otherwise.

7.5.7 Objective function: Probability maximization

The optimization journey started with an initial space Φ_U of quasi-random potential allocations, reduced the dataset to a space of quasi-random Ψ_U admissible compositions, and further reduced the set to the risk-adequate initial allocations Θ_U. Thus, the objective function can now be imposed on the risk/return properties of the portfolios contained in Θ_U. The total return distribution of the investment returns over time which entered the optimization exercise can be plotted on digital tools without any discrepancy between the optimal asset allocation and the operational portfolio.

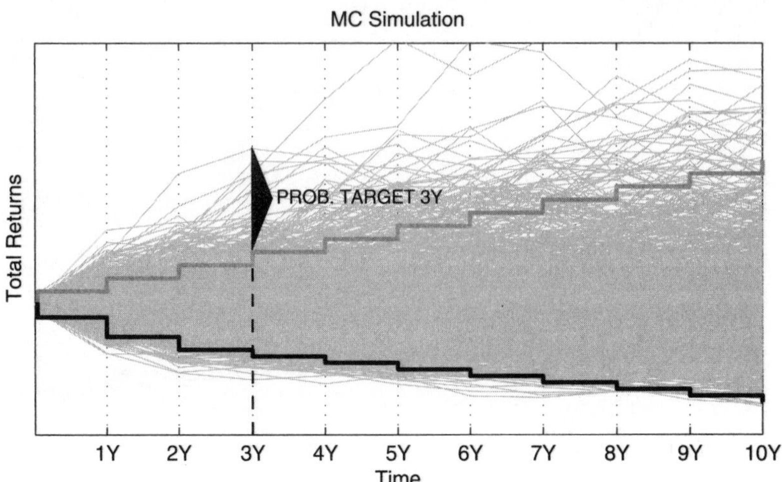

FIGURE 7.10 Example of Monte Carlo simulation

Figure 7.10 shows a Monte Carlo simulation and the overlapping of the ambition line and the risk limit.

The optimization problem can be performed in the multi-period where $t \in \Gamma$. Hence, one needs to have a notion of preference that determines at which level of the target function a particular point in time dominates another. This can be achieved by introducing a multi-period weighting scheme K which is a vector of $k \in K$ that allocates a positive weight at each $t \in \Gamma$. The weighting scheme is phrased rather generally and need not necessarily integrate to 1, since it might incorporate a normalization of the target function over time as well. Alternatively, one could estimate a more refined indicator of the multi-period probability by computing at the final investment horizon the conditional probability of reaching such a final step given the probability measurement at all previous allocation steps.

The process can be summarized in Table 7.1.

Objective function: maximize the probability of complying with a minimum, time-dependent ambition or target return λ_U^A, subject to a multi-period weighting scheme K over a time horizon Γ and across all elements in Θ_U, so that:

$$\Theta^*_{U,S,\Gamma} : \max_{\Theta} \left\{ \sum_{t \in \Gamma} k_t P_{U,S,t} \left(R > \lambda_t^A \right) \right\} \tag{7.28}$$

in which, λ_Γ^A is the ambition line expressed as a total return function over the investment horizon Γ:

$$\lambda_\Gamma^A : \left\{ \lambda_t | t \in \Gamma \right\} \tag{7.29}$$

TABLE 7.1 The PSO Process

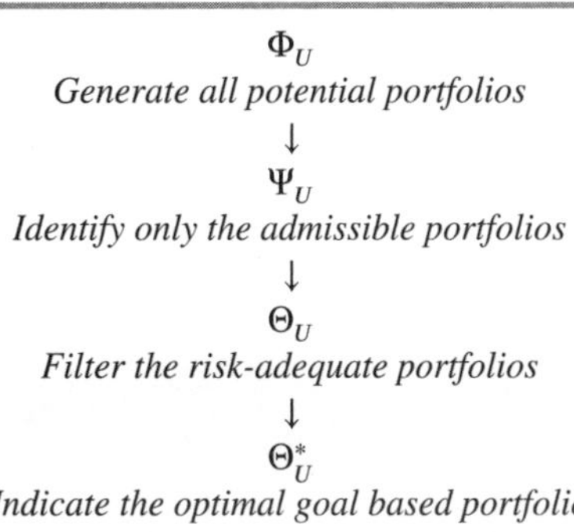

Φ_U

Generate all potential portfolios

↓

Ψ_U

Identify only the admissible portfolios

↓

Θ_U

Filter the risk-adequate portfolios

↓

Θ_U^*

Indicate the optimal goal based portfolio

Clearly, the multi-period optimization can be turned into a discrete or single point in time optimization by assigning full weight to a discrete set of points or a single point only. However, if the weight is not allocated to a single point only, the construction of the weighting scheme should reflect the nature of the respective variable and its term structure to allow for meaningful results.

The probability measures, such as the probability of beating the investment goal or of falling short of the risk appetite limit, can be plotted for the optimal or any other portfolio (as in Figure 7.11).

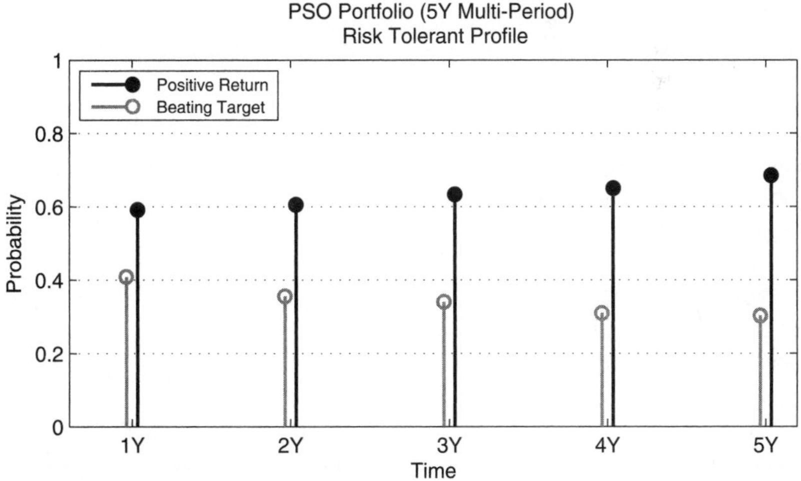

FIGURE 7.11 Example of probability measurement

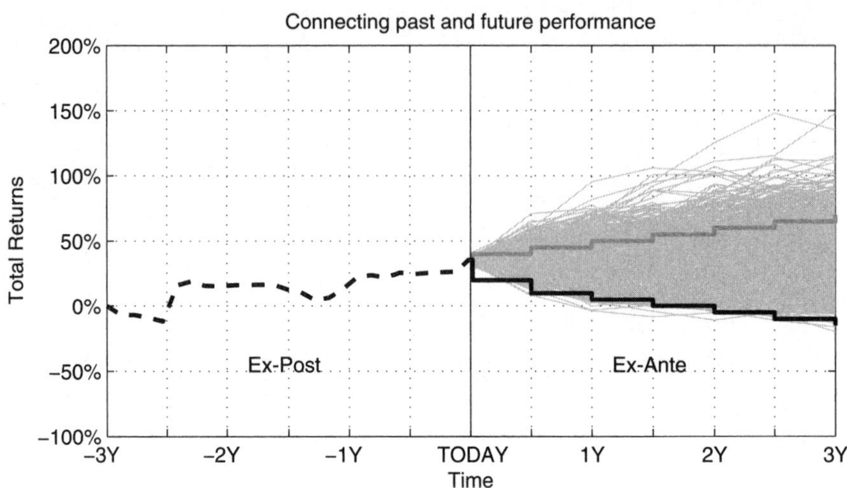

FIGURE 7.12 Example of GBI performance reporting

Robo-Advisors performance over time can also be investigated to highlight whether the investment goals are still attainable, have been achieved, or are challenged by adverse market movements (as in Figure 7.12).

Robo-Advisors can indicate minimum probability targets for each time step and verify ex-ante and ex-post the compliance of both the strategic and the tactical asset allocations with the ambitions and risk appetite of final investors. This allows us to anticipate the needs for a proactive revision of the asset allocation, in case the investment has performed better than expected, as the market turned in favour of the elected strategy (indicating the possibility of cashing in and entering into a new portfolio to enhance investment returns) or in case the investment has under performed, as the market turned against the elected strategy or might not provide enough drift or volatility to achieve the stated ambition within the investment horizon (indicating the need to revise the asset allocation and optimize the timing of such a decision).

An appealing feature of PSO is that we can operate multiple problems without having to recalibrate the full set of simulation inputs: we can redefine time horizons, time steps, allocation constraints, client ambitions, or risk appetite levels and operate on the same stochastic distribution of the total returns of individual products. This should facilitate the institutionalization of the methodology across advisory networks, well outside the specialized desks of quantitative professionals, hence allowing sell-side institutions to deliver better and more transparent support to buy-side players. Moreover, we can identify an intuitive metric that permits us to compare strategic and tactical asset allocations with a certain level of intuition. Probability is such a measure, such as the probability of beating a financial goal, of yielding a minimum total return, or avoiding a capital loss.

7.5.8 Final remarks on PSO

PSO is a fairly unrestricted framework based on exhaustive enumeration that can encompass a large variety of optimization exercises in terms of:

- timeline discretization;
- definition of the risk limit (e.g., VaR, Worst Case, Tail-Loss);
- definition of the ambition (e.g., total return, asset value, income stream);
- definition of the objective function (e.g., maximum probability of achieving a return target, maximum probability of affording an annuity);
- a different combination of ambitions, risk tolerances, and time discretization.

In particular, the framework is suited to meaningful stress test analysis of operational and model portfolios because it is based on scenario analysis. Economic cycles can be conveniently modelled over time to test the robustness of investment policies and rebalancing assumptions, which can be a relevant input to Gamification exercises.

7.5.9 Conclusions

Goal Based Investing seeks to facilitate the implementation of investment policies which are more transparent and consistent with individual preferences and long-term ambitions. The probability of reaching or falling short of an investment target becomes a mainstream indicator to establish the adequacy of model portfolios with regard to individual ambitions and risk tolerance. Markowitz and his co-authors (Das et al., 2011) have recently innovated beyond the original Mean-Variance and Black-Litterman propositions, by replacing the standard deviation with the shortfall probability measure. Probabilistic Scenario Optimization provides a more flexible and consistent framework for the maximization of goal probabilities in the multi-period, within a risk constrained scenario simulation framework. The adoption of probabilistic scenarios requires thorough understanding of modern risk management techniques, based upon full revaluation methods of actual securities by means of multi-period stochastic simulations. The next chapter discusses scenario analysis in the context of educational Gamification, which is a relevant example of sustaining innovation that can enhance Robo-Advisors' propositions, and facilitate the understanding of the impact of personal investment behaviour with regard to otherwise complex investment decisions.

CHAPTER 8

Goal Based Investing and Gamification

"Before starting, agree upon a definite hour of termination, when the richest player will be declared the winner."

—Monopoly, Parker Brothers (1930)

This chapter drafts the principles and mechanics of Gamification, which is more art than science, and could allow digital wealth managers to modernize the steps of risk profiling by testing investors' appetite for risk, help them understand the impact of uncertainty on portfolio returns, enhance compliance, reduce attrition during a market downturn and rewire investors' brains toward more consistent investment behaviours, and hence pursue personal goals with more emotional clarity.

8.1 INTRODUCTION

Millennials use technology differently than older generations: they use mobile devices more than laptops, they communicate with chats more than emails, they play digital games. Playing games is a fundamental attribute of humans, though shared in many forms by many animals, particularly in their formative months because it fosters learning by means of innocent experiences. Nowadays, Gamification is also a powerful method to achieve sustained innovation in financial services because it can provide a way for individuals to rewire their brains and bodies and achieve better investment behaviour against the imprints generated by financial events and the experience of their formative years. Moreover Robo-Advisors and digital wealth managers could find innovative ways to elicit investors' profiles and replace questionnaires with engaging experiences, and track individuals' behaviour and decision-making during their digital game to derive personality insights.

8.2 PRINCIPLES OF GAMIFICATION

Gamification is a way to improve productivity by working with the right mix of negative and positive emotions, challenges and rewards, a sense of accomplishment, and in some cases strengthened peering and social relationships. It is quite an innovative field of digital technology when applied to banking, aiming to take the essential ingredients of games and apply them to real world financial situations, such as saving, investing, and retiring. The idea of enhancing the theoretical knowledge and practical skills of individuals by engaging them with video games has a recognized antecedent in the aviation industry, which has utilized flight simulators to train pilots on strength simulations for many decades. Flight simulators allow verification of experts' knowledge and test their skills in a way that supports their optimal behaviour and reactivity when confronting unusual situations. The financial services industry has just started to learn how to train its professional workforce, for example with gaming sessions for financial advisors, but also how to provide long-tail customers with engaging user experiences to improve their investment behaviour, create stickiness, and enhance profitability.

Financial Gamification can be a powerful mechanism to learn how to tame emotions in order to size up higher return opportunities, face the potential realization of risks and losses, decide which risk management action seems better suited to mitigate them, and most of all visualize how uncertainty can affect our beliefs beyond personal knowledge, professional expectations, and measurable risk. Therefore, Gamification helps to stress test investment strategies, anticipate the consequences of a downturn on portfolio performance and asset allocations, and create an experience that customers can revert to if they need to stay invested during a market crash. All in all, individuals can verify the best mix of actions to improve the probability of achieving their financial goals, as single mental bets or within holistic experiences. Hence, Gamification speaks the language of Goal Based Investing and sits squarely at the crossroads between digital technology, behavioural finance, and motivation theory. Its capability to help individuals modify their investment behaviour is an attractive feature in facilitating the revolution in investment perspective advocated by Goal Based Investing, and learning to focus on the best actions towards an individual's goals rather than greed and fear stemming from attempts to tame the markets.

In fact, this innovation is not about learning new concepts, although it would definitely foster the financial education of the player, but rather experiencing the consequences of personal decisions when confronting expected and unexpected situations, thus the interaction between risk and uncertainty. Although grounded in scientific research and psychology, Gamification is much more an art than science, because it involves many elements of design, imagination, and emotional interaction

TABLE 8.1 Differences between promotional marketing and Gamification

Promotional Marketing	Gamification
About sales	About user experience
Rewards to induce single activities	Change of clients' behaviour to create stickiness
Short life span	Long-term commitment

which set it apart from well defined and replicable techniques. Most importantly, it should not be confused with promotional marketing, which is about sales and seeks to encourage a well defined action by means of a reward (as explained in Table 8.1). The scope of Gamification is not to give rewards or prizes to induce one-time consumption of a service or a product, such as opening an account. It attempts to engage individuals with the right mix of frustration and pride to induce a change in long-term behaviour and provide digital wealth managers with a reasonable stickiness in their clients' attitudes. In essence, it is about the user experience and hopes to attain the desired behaviour of the players by leveraging psychology to enhance their satisfaction.

Therefore, financial Gamification is about investors doing things differently and better. It is based on two main principles: continuous engagement and investment behaviour:

- **continuous engagement:** investors are invited to stay tuned and engaged by using game mechanics, as a way to enhance loyalty, favour cross-selling, focus on relevant news, and filter noise.
- **investment behaviour:** players are encouraged to play and learn the optimal game strategy, which ultimately corresponds to the optimal allocation of their ambitions, savings, investments, consumption levels and, last but not least, their fears.

The strategic focus on long-term customer behaviour explains the strong link to the theory of motivation and behavioural finance. Goal Based Investing Gamification does not focus on myopic motivators such as prizes, bonuses, or discounts. What matters are the intrinsic motivators of individuals. This is about their need for financial security, their aspiration to become, their desire to belong to a group. Successful Gamification requires a deep understanding of the multiple patterns of investment behaviour by focusing on emotional and graphical representation more than financial concepts and explanations. Therefore, the Probabilistic Scenario Optimization framework is well suited to act as the engine of Goal Based Investing Gamification, because it can provide the consistent simulation of real-world scenarios to create a graphical representation of the interaction between investment decision-making and otherwise complex market events and mathematical relationships.

Undoubtedly, games are a very attractive experience for human beings of all ages, not just children but also adults. The reason why games are so attractive to human beings is because they are about an engaging attempt to achieve well defined goals, and the learning of the best strategies and behaviours to attain them. Therefore, the ultimate financial innovation comes from achieving a transformational journey back to the roots of our human behaviour, which is not about rational investments but emotional decision-making, and rewiring our brains away from greed and fear, focusing on our real selves and motivations.

8.3 GAMIFICATION OF WEALTH MANAGEMENT

Robo-Advisors are digital tools targeting new investment behaviours, hence they would be naturally positioned to embrace Gamification. However, it is recommended that innovators carefully research their offers and the nature of the existing and prospective client base to identify how Gamification can fit into the processes. Being a long-term engagement, successful Gamification needs to be ingrained in conscious business and branding strategies, because it is intended to create emotional stickiness with customers and to last as business evolves, markets transform, and people change. Although a cost effective way to achieve innovation, not all wealth management offers can be unbundled into a gamified proposition. Hunter and Werbach (2012) have identified four criteria to guide decision-makers in the choice. Such products or services must be linked to a set of intrinsic motivators and gaming actions need to be meaningful; algorithms exist to model customer actions and their consequences and gaming experiences can reconcile conflicts within the prepotency of motivations. Thus, the following questions need to be answered:

- **Motivation:** where could a digital wealth manager derive value from encouraging the investment behaviour of actual clients?
- **Meaningful choices:** are the target activities related to advised products and services sufficiently interesting?
- **Structure:** can the desired investment behaviour be modelled through a set of algorithms?
- **Potential conflicts:** can the game avoid conflicts within the existing motivational structure of individuals?

We have discussed in previous chapters the relevance of the hierarchy of motivations and the corresponding wealth allocation framework, as a key factor to shape investment decision-making of taxable investors. It follows the emotional relevance of safety, peering, and aspiring. Money is an emotional thing, unlike electrons. Therefore, most actions directed to saving, investing, or retiring have a high level of motivational bias. Clearly, not all individuals exhibit the same, given their personal or generational values, family constraints, accumulated wealth, and biological propensity for risk-taking. Many individuals might believe that financial markets are not interesting, and that the impact of financial variables on everyday life is not relevant. Quite the contrary. The price of oil can affect economies, hence growth prospects of firms and families. Quantitative easing can reverberate into bull markets and the build-up of damaging bubbles. Knowingly or unknowingly, most of personal savings dedicated to retirement are nowadays linked to the cycles of financial markets (e.g., Australian superannuation funds).

Therefore, activities like retirement planning are becoming extremely relevant for a very large portion of the population, making Robo-Retirement Gamification a competitive breakthrough to engage taxable investors with meaningful and intuitive propositions. Philanthropy and investing with purpose, such as peer-to-peer lending to African households, can also be relevant for socially conscious individuals and provide the emotional leverage which Gamification can exploit. Since individuals are not identical, personalization remains a must, which Gamification can foster by inviting players to engage as avatars, whose attributes are tailored around actual individuals or their aspirations.

With regard to the use of algorithms, Robo-Advisors have already demonstrated the relevance of automated rebalancing for long-term investing, and Probabilistic Scenario Optimization has presented the advantages of working with scenarios to create meaningful simulations of risks and uncertainties.

As we have already learned, working with goals means working with conflicting mental accounts. Some goals refer to short-term necessities, others to long-term aspirations. In particular, individuals seem to be continuously trapped in the asset management perspective which encourages them to focus on myopic satisfaction as opposed to long-term investing. The conflict between short-term reward (e.g., myopic trading) and long-term benefits (e.g., automatic rebalancing of passive investment strategies) can be reconciled by means of Gamification.

We have discussed in previous chapters the relevance and the perils of the use of questionnaires to profile investors. Gamification could be a powerful diagnostic to detect ex-ante the potential behaviour of individuals when confronted with difficult financial decisions, such as stay the course during a downturn, rebalance when markets are rallying or confront return expectations with negative rates. The behaviour of an individual during a digital game could be tracked and reviewed by analytics to detect personality insights, reported and stored for compliance as part of more advanced processes of know your customer.

8.4 THE MECHANICS OF GAMES

Gamification and promotional marketing are different because while marketing works on one side only of the emotional equation, that is reward, Gamification operates on the dark side of the game as well, that is pain. We have learned from behavioural finance that individuals are very asymmetrical in the perceptions of pleasure and pain stemming from financial gains and losses of the same magnitude. We have also learned that individuals wire experience through their emotional background and create personal biases based on life events and experiences during their formative years. Gamification can provide a way to rewire our brains and the way we engage emotionally by promoting new experiences that help to change investment habits and feelings. A well-designed Gamification experience would ignite players' emotions and craft an adequate balance between frustration (e.g., simulation of a financial loss) and price (e.g., achievement of a financial goal). This can be done by working on rules, challenges, and rewards. Rules create the boundaries that investors are invited to explore. For example, what would happen if we broke up portfolio diversification and piled up idiosyncratic risk, what if we kept high stocks of cash when inflation skyrocketed, or we lost our job but did not have any form of insurance to help us pay the mortgage? Challenges create the progressive engagement that encourages us to test our skills though we are uncertain of what comes next, and hence fail or succeed but always learn, stay tuned, and adapt. Rewards grant us the pride we deserve for having defined the best strategy to invest with awareness, that is being conscious of the perils. While reward mechanics take the form of points that we can share with peers, or more advanced leaderboards we can access, or virtual goods we are offered, the focus is directed to impacting our basic human motivations such as status, recognition, and self-expression. To succeed, goals need to be clear and progress needs to be monitored continuously to diagnose performance and provide feedback to achieve higher levels of mastery, as indicated by the player journey in Herger (2014) and sketched out in Figure 8.1. Therefore, games will provide scaffolding mechanisms, prompting hints, suggestions, or partial solutions to keep players progressing.

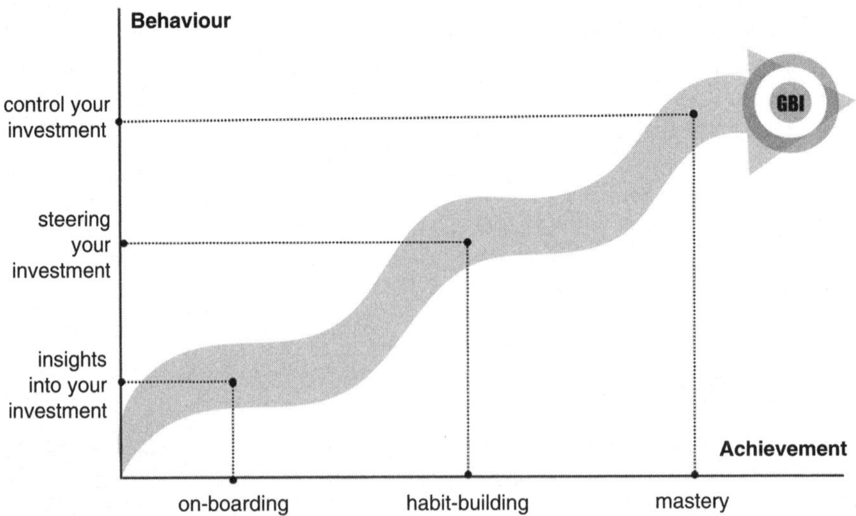

FIGURE 8.1 The player journey

People enjoy games and keep on playing even when they fail, to get better and better at them because they can provide motivation even after failure. Therefore, they can equip us with contextual bridging, closing the gap between theory and life.

8.5 CONCLUSIONS

Gamification in banking and finance benefits from Goal Based Investing and behavioural finance, whose principles provide guidance to game mechanics. The potential capability of Gamification to help individuals modify their investment behaviour is an attractive feature to facilitate the digital revolution in the investment perspective advocated by this book. Although still visionary, Goal Based Investing Gamification could be the ultimate case of innovation at the crossroad between FINance and TECHnology.

Concluding Remarks

Working at the intersection between finance and technology is an incredible experience which requires patience and imagination because professionals operating in these fields have different skill sets and speak different languages. Most of this book was written during flights, after meetings with clients and prospects, banking technologists, senior advisors, friends, marketing officers, rampant entrepreneurs, colleagues, wealthy investors and families. I am indebted to all of them: after almost every meeting and conversation I was able to add a new piece to the puzzle. The chance to share ideas is the richest asset that innovators possess, as no mass market revolutionary vision can be the result of a thinker working in isolation. However, the world is noisy and it is not easy to discern a rationale in an irrational age, and provide a consistent reading of all the disruptive changes which are sweeping the wealth management industry. There is no innovation without a strategy for innovation, which this book, in a very humble way, has attempted to help craft. Most of this book invites the reader to review the underlying forces which foster transformation in wealth management, but and not only to look at the surface of the vibrant FinTech ecosystem; it invites the reader to see that TECH innovation brought forward by today's Robo-Advisors is incomplete without and equivalent FIN innovation about scenario analysis and portfolio construction. The book spells out a vision for the future of personal banking in which clients' needs take centre stage, gamification helps them learn how to make better investment decisions, and the industry thrives in a more symmetrical, transparent and risk-controlled landscape. The goal was to offer a narrative that was not prescriptive but sincerely descriptive and searching. Transforming a bank is not an easy task, and launching a FinTech entity is not only fun. But one thing that I learned during sailing classes in my formative years, is that one cannot always reach one's destination via a straight route. Often one needs to deviate from the target destination to gain speed, exploit the winds, and work out the currents. Recognizing the forces of nature and how they may help or hinder our progress is the first step. Attuning to the elements is the second, whether they are water, wind, temperature or the shape of the waves. Mastering the crew, the boat, and its technology is the last, although by no means the least important. The rest is passion and determination. And sometimes luck will help too! I hope that you enjoy your journey and that a heartfelt "good luck" from the author as well as his book aids you in achieving your goals.

Bibliography

Arnott, Robert D., Berkin, Andrew L. and Ye, Jia (2000) How Well Have Taxable Investors Been Served in the 1980's and 1990's?, *First Quadrant*, 3.

Barberis, Nicholas (2000) Investing in the Long Run when Returns are Predictable, *The Journal of Finance*, 55(1), 225–264.

Bertsimas, Dimitris, Lauprete, Geoffrey J. and Samarov, Alexander (2004) Shortfall as a Risk Measure: Properties Optimization and Applications, *Journal of Economic Dynamics & Control*, 28, 1353–1381.

Biondi, Luca (2013) *Il Modello Black and Litterman: Descrizione Teorica del modello*, Edizioni Accademiche Italiane.

Black, Fischer and Litterman, Robert (1992) Global Portfolio Optimization, *Financial Analysts Journal*, 48(1), 68–74.

Bogle, John C. (2009) *Common Sense on Mutual Funds*, John Wiley & Sons.

Brown, Jeffrey R., Ivković, Zoran, Smith, Paul A. and Weisbenner, Scott (2008) Neighbors Matter: Causal Community Effects and Stock Market Participation, *The Journal of Finance*, 63(3), 1509–1531.

Brunel, Jean L. P. (2002) *Integrated Wealth Management: The New Direction for Portfolio Managers*, Euromoney Books.

Brunel, Jean L. P. (2003) Revisiting the Asset Allocation Challenge Through a Behavioral Finance Lens, *The Journal of Wealth Management*, 6(2 Fall), 10–20.

Brunel, Jean L. P. (2015) *Goals-Based Wealth Management: An Integrated and Practical Approach to Changing the Structure of Wealth Advisory Practices*, Wiley Finance.

Burns, William J. and Slovic, Paul (2012) Modeling the Dynamics of Risk Perception and Fear: Examining Amplifying Mechanisms and Their Consequences, Research Project Summaries, Paper 104.

Campbell, John Y. and Viceira, Luis M. (2002) *Strategic Asset Allocation: Portfolio Choice for Long-Term Investors*, Oxford University Press.

Cerulli Associates (2013) *The Cerulli Report: Understanding and Addressing a More Sophisticated Population*, Cerulli Associates.

Chhabra, Ashvin B. (2005) Beyond Markowitz: A Comprehensive Wealth Allocation Framework for Individual Investors, *The Journal of Wealth Management*, 7(4), 8–34.

Chhabra, Ashvin B. (2011) The Wealth Allocation Framework Revisited, Merrill Lynch Wealth Management Institute White Paper.

Chhabra, Ashvin B. (2015) *The Aspirational Investor: Taming the Markets to Achieve Your Life's Goals*, HarperBusiness.

Christensen, Clayton M. (2002) *The Innovator's Dilemma*, Collins.

Christensen, Clayton M. and Raynor, Michael E. (2003) *The Innovator's Solution*, Harvard Business School Publishing Corporation.

Coates, John (2013) *The Hour Between Dog and Wolf: Risk Taking, Gut Feelings and the Biology of Boom and Bust*, Penguin Books.

Credit Suisse (2012) *Global Wealth Databook 2012*, Credit Suisse Research Institute.

Das, Sanjiv, Markowitz, Harry, Scheid, Jonathan and Statman, Meir (2010) Portfolio Optimization with Mental Accounts, *Journal of Financial and Quantitative Analysis*, 45(2), 311–334.

Das, Sanjiv, Markowitz, Harry, Scheid, Jonathan and Statman, Meir (2011) Portfolios for Investors Who Want to Reach Their Goals While Staying on the Mean/Variance Efficient Frontier, *The Journal of Wealth Management*, 14(2), 25–31.

Dembo, Ron (1991) Scenario Optimization, *Annals of Operations Research*, 30(1–4), 63–80.

Dembo, Ron and King, Alan (1992) Tracking Models and the Optimal Regret Distribution in Asset Allocation, *Applied Stochastic Models and Data Analysis*, 8(3), 151–157.

Dembo, Ron and Freeman, Andrew (1998) *Seeing Tomorrow: Rewriting the Rules of Risk*, John Wiley & Sons.

Drobetz, Wolfgang, Oertmann, Peter and Zimmerman, Heinz (2003) *Global Asset Allocation: New Methods and Applications*, Wiley Finance.

Elton, Edwin J. and Gruber, Martin J. (1995) *Modern Portfolio Theory and Investment Analysis*, 5th edition, John Wiley & Sons.

Estrada, Javier (2008) Mean-Semivariance Optimization: A Heuristic Approach, *Journal of Applied Finance*, 18(1), 57–72.

Faure, Henri (1982) Discrépance de suites associées á un systéme de numération (en dimensions), *Acta Arithmetica*, 41(4), 337–351.

Foerster, Stephen, Linnainmaa, Juhani T., Melzer, Brian T. and Previtero, Alessandro (2014) Retail Financial Advice: Does One Size Fit All? National Bureau of Economic Research Working Paper 20712.

Fox, Craig R., Ratner, Rebecca K. and Lieb, Daniel S. (2005) How Subjective Grouping of Options Influences Choice and Allocation: Diversification Bias and the Phenomenon of Partition Dependence, *Journal of Experimental Psychology: General*, 134(4), 538–551.

Gilli, Manfred, Këllezi, Evis and Hysi, Hilda (2002) A Data-Driven Optimization Heuristic for Downside Risk Minimization, Swiss Finance Institute Research Paper no. 6.

Gofman, Michael and Manela, Asaf (2012) *An Empirical Evaluation of the Black-Litterman Approach to Portfolio Choice*, available at SSRN: http://ssrn.com/abstract=1782033.

Halton, John H. (1960) On the Efficiency of Certain Quasi-Random Sequences of Points in Evaluating Multi-Dimensional Integrals 2, *Numerische Mathematik*, 84–90.

Herger, Mario (2014) *Gamification in Banking & Finance, Enterprise Gamification*, CreateSpace Independent Publishing Platform.

Huelin, Lars and Mirza, Kheyam (2011) *Portfolio Optimization in a Downside Risk Framework: A Study of the Performance of Downside Risk Measures in Investment Management*, Lap Lambert Academic Publishing.

Hunter, Dan and Werbach, Kevin (2012) *For the Win*, Wharton Digital Press.

Idzorek, Thomas M. (2004) *A Step-by-Step Guide to the Black-Litterman Model: Incorporating user-specified confidence intervals.*

Idzorek, Thomas M. and Xiong, James X. (2010) *Mean-Variance Versus Mean-Conditional Value-at-Risk Optimization: The Impact of Incorporating Fat Tails and Skewness into the Asset Allocation Decision*, Ibbotson.

Investment Company Institute (2015) *Investment Company Fact Book 2015: A Review of Trends and Activities in the U.S. Investment Company Industry*, 55th edition, ICI.

Janssen, Ronald, Kramer, Bert and Boender, Guus (2013) Life Cycle Investing: From Target-Date to Goal-Based Investing, *The Journal of Wealth Management*, 16, 23–32.

Jones, Charles M. (2002) *A Century of Stock Market Liquidity and Trading Costs*, Graduate School of Business, Columbia University.

Kahneman, Daniel and Tversky, Amos (1979) Prospect Theory: An Analysis of Decision under Risk, *Econometrica*, 47, 263–291.

Keynes, John M. (1931) *Essays in Persuasion*, Macmillan.

Klement, Joachim (2015) Investor Risk Profiling: An Overview, CFA Institute Research Foundation Briefs.

Klement, Joachim, and Miranda, R. E. (2012) Kicking the Habit: How Experience Determines Financial Risk Preferences, *The Journal of Wealth Management*, 15(2), 10–25.

Laney, Douglas (2001) *3D Data Management: Controlling Data Volume, Velocity, and Variety*, Meta Group.

Lintner, John (1965) The Valuation of Risk Assets and the Selection of Risky Investments in Stock Portfolios and Capital Budgets, *Review of Economics and Statistics*, 47(1), 13–37.

Litterman, Robert and He, Guangliang (1999) *The Intuition Behind Black-Litterman Model Portfolios*, Goldman Sachs Investment Management Division.

Malkiel, Burton G. and Ellis, Charles D. (2013) *The Elements of Investing*, John Wiley & Sons.

Markowitz, Harry M. (1990) *Judgment under Uncertainty: Heuristic and Biases*, Baruch College at The City University of New York.

Markowitz, Harry M. (1952) Portfolio Selection 7, *The Journal of Finance*, 77–91.

Martellini, Lionel and Ziemann, Volker (2007) *Extending Black-Litterman Analysis Beyond the Mean-Variance Framework*, EDHEC Risk and Asset Management Research Centre.

Maslow, Abraham H. (1943) A Theory of Human Motivation, *Psychological Review*, 50, 370–396.

Maude, David (2010) *Global Private Banking and Wealth Management: The New Realities*, John Wiley & Sons.

Melnick, Edward L., Nayyar, Praveen R., Pinedo, Michael L. and Seshadri, Sridhar (2000) *Creating Value for the Financial Services*, Springer.

Michaud, Richard O., Esch, David N. and Michaud, Robert O. (2013) Deconstructing Black-Litterman: How to Get the Portfolio You Already Knew You Wanted, *Journal of Investment Management*, 11(1), 6–20.

MyPrivateBanking (2014) *Robo-Advisors: Threats and Opportunities for the Global Wealth Management Industry*, MyPrivateBanking Research.

MyPrivateBanking (2015) *Robo-Advisors 2.0: How Automated Investing is Infiltrating the Wealth Management Industry*, MyPrivateBanking Research.

Niederreiter, Harald (1987) *Random Number Generation and Quasi-Monte Carlo Methods*, CBMS-NSF Regional Conference Series in Applied Mathematics.

Rha, Jong-Youn, Montalto, Catherine P. and Hanna, Sherman D. (2006) The Effect of Self-Control Mechanisms on Household Saving Behavior, *Financial Counselling and Planning*, 17(2).

Rice, Douglas (2005) Variance in Risk Tolerant Measurement: Towards a Uniform Theory, PhD Dissertation Golden Gate University.

Rockafellar, Tyrrel R. and Uryasev, Stanislav (2000) Optimization of Conditional Value at Risk, *Journal of Risk*, 2(3), 21–41.

Shafir, Eldar, and Thaler, Richard H. (2006) Invest Now, Drink Later, Spend Never: On the mental accounting of delayed consumption, *Journal of Economic Psychology*, 27, 694–712.

Sharpe, William F. (1964) Capital Asset Prices: A Theory of Market Equilibrium under Conditions of Risk, *The Journal of Finance*, 19(3), 425–442.

Shefrin, Hersh and Statman, Meir (2000) Behavioural Portfolio Theory, *Journal of Financial and Quantitative Analysis*, 35(2), 127–151.

Sironi, Paolo (2015) *Modern Portfolio Management: From Markowitz to Probabilistic Scenario Optimisation*, Risk Books.

Sobol, Ilya (1967) On the distribution of points in a cube and the approximate evaluation of integrals, *USSR Computational Mathematics and Mathematical Physics*, 7(4), 86–112.

Swensen, David F. (2005) *Unconventional Success: A Fundamental Approach to Personal Investment*, Free Press.

Talent Management Team – Executive Office – United Nations Joint Staff Pension Fund (2013) *Traditionalists, Baby Boomers, Generation X, Generation Y (and Generation Z) Working Together. What Matters and How They Learn? How different are they? Fact or Fiction.*

Thaler, Richard H. (1990) Anomalies: Saving, Fungibility and Mental Accounts, *The Journal of Economic Perspectives*, 4(1), 193–205.

Walters, Jay (2009) *The Black-Litterman Model in Detail.*

Weber, Martin, Weber, Elke U. and Nosic, Alen (2012) Who Takes Risks When and Why: Determinants of Changes in Investor Risk Taking, *Review of Finance*, 17, 847–883.

Index

Index compiled by Indexing Specialists (UK) Ltd